THE GULF COAST BOYS

A Memoir

RICHARD J. DOBSON

Other Books by Richard J. Dobson

Pleasures of the High Rhine: A Texas Singer in Exile

The Years the Wind Blew Away—Don Ricardo's Life and Times
The Newsletters of Richard J. Dobson

THE GULF COAST BOYS

A MEMOIR

RICHARD J. DOBSON

The Gulf Coast Boys
Second Edition
© 2013 Richard J. Dobson

All rights reserved.

Print ISBN: 978-1-4935898-1-4

Richard Dobson
Schmiedgasse 4
CH-8253 Diessenhofen
Switzerland
Tel. +41 52 654 1017
saltysongs@bluewin.ch
www.richard-j-dobson.ch

Book design: Sonya Unrein

CONTENTS

The Beach	9
Camille and the Reverend Billy Graham	12
Born Again	16
Music City	19
The Boys	26
New Year's Day	32
Day Tripping	37
Jackson Farewell	40
Denver	44
Moving On	47
Crested Butte	51
One Long Day	54
Texas Bound	59
Uncle Seymour	64
Some Changes	67
Island Days	72
The Part Time	75
Jaws	78
Endangered Species	81
Gandalf's	84
September Logs	87
Chef Rex	92
September Logs II	94
Making Tracks	97
Nashville	104
A Lateral Move	108
Holly	110
Galley Hands	113
Farewell Uncle Seymour	120
Daddy Bill	123

Rig Logs	128
The Key	133
Kerrville	136
Changing Partners	139
In Texas Last December	143
The Reaper Collects	148
The Shipyard	152
A Regrettable Episode	155
The Rabbit	158
Outward Bound	160
Grass Fires	164
Crossing Over	166
Country Matters	170
Scotland	175
Homeward Bound	180
Zapata	182
Bad Magic At Gilley's	185
The Blessed Event	189
How It's Done/Not Done	191
Dada Kontrol	193
The *Melissa*	195
The Big Taste	199
Trouble	204
Home Owners	208
Old Wood	211
The Bear	214
Post Script	216
Bolivar Redux	220
1998–Special Thanks	222

The Beach

The barrier island chain off the Texas coast runs roughly northeast to southwest from Galveston down towards Mexico. Galveston, one of the more inhabited parts, stretches from the Bolivar Roads and the Houston Ship Channel thirty-two miles down to San Luis pass. It was once an important place until, early this century, the channel was dug. I first began this tale from some notes written on a scrap of paper, then transcribed it on a garage sale word processor that didn't last a month. Such is the way with machines. We are online with one now and pray it sees us through with the task.

I was smoking marijuana from an improvised bong made from a Sprite can, waiting to take a walk on the beach were a few people were still out strolling and looking for shells, though most had already packed up and gone back up to Houston. I wanted the place to myself, just me and the birds. Earlier, the boy and I had driven out to the east end of the Island and parked where we could watch the shop traffic.

"What are we doing here?"

"I just want to watch the boats awhile."

"Oh." He pondered this. My kid, a BOI, or, born-on-the-island. I could tell he had adopted the attitude common to the natives who routinely avoid Seawall Boulevard because of the tourists.

I was looking out over the channel, thinking of all the times we'd run in and out of there with Rex (or Wrecks, as he sometimes calls himself) and Captain Johnny Howard on the *Part*

Time and of all those other leaking, wooden-hulled shrimp trawlers. Then later, on the sleek, aluminum-hulled *Alpha One*, all speed and flash with three roaring v-12 Detroit Diesels making hotshot runs out to the offshore oil platforms and drilling rigs. I was thinking of the fishing we did from those boats, and of all the snapper, kingfish, bonita, and shark we pulled in. And I was trying to imagine earlier times, days I was not there to witness, just a second ago in the larger span of things.

Looking a mile or so across to the Bolivar side, we could just see the north jetty and the old lighthouse where Jane Long, said to be the first white woman to come to this part of the country, scared away a war party of Karankawa Indians approaching by canoe from the Island. She, her young daughter, Annie, and her slave woman, Kian, had been left a cannon with which to defend themselves. Jane was pregnant. They had been abandoned there by her husband, who had gone off on a filibustering adventure to Mexico.

The women managed to survive, living off their dwindling supplies and fish, which were incredibly plentiful in those days. They were eventually rescued after the terrible winter of 1821-22, when the bay froze over. They benefitted from an enormous fish kill, some of which they were able to scoop out and preserve in brine. In Jane Long's account, they watched a bear cross the ice to the Island.

That was yesterday, and we can only imagine what became of the bear. If time could be switched to fast-forward like a tape machine, we might think of the days, the seasons, and the years going by like high-pitched blips of sound. Like strobe-flashes as they might appear from a great distance: Jean Laffite and his pirates are here. The Karankawa retreat but return again. Jane and her party are rescued, only to learn of the death of her husband, James Long (a surgeon under Andrew Jackson at the Battle of New Orleans), killed down in Mexico. More settlers arrive, coming overland from Tennessee. Inland, Davy Crockett, William Travis, James Bowie, and 185 more die after a ten-day siege at the Alamo on March 6, 1836. Three hundred and forty-two more under Colonel James Fannin are treacherously massacred at Goliad on the twenty-seventh. The Mexicans under General Santa Anna finally get their comeuppance at the battle of San Jacinto. Galveston becomes a port to rival New Orleans and an entry point for more Europeans, one of whom was this boy's ancestor.

The kid brought me back. "Hey Dad, can I have a Coke?"

"Sure. Do you want something to eat?"

"No thanks. Just a Coke will be fine."

We stopped at Nash's Bait Camp across the road. Blue-eyed and weather-beaten, Mr. Nash had been there ever since I started coming back to the Island in the early seventies. Demolished by storms and patched back together, it's one of those places where old guys gather to drink beer and pass the afternoons. But I never saw Mr. Nash selling any bait. The boy and I headed back toward town where I dropped him off at his mom's house.

Back at the beach house I smoked and waited for the sunset. I read somewhere that the Karankawa used to wade in the surf and stand, arms outstretched toward the sun. They had come back to the Island after Laffite and his men decamped for unknown destinations. Presumably they did not realize when they were fired upon that the mud fort was being defended by two women and a young girl who had raised a red petticoat for a flag. The Karankawa were tall for Indians, well over six feet. They did not leave much behind them, and little is known of their origins.

Camille and the Reverend Billy Graham

I think it was Camille that came ashore and tore up the Texas coast back in September, 1971. In any case, it had a woman's name, as all hurricanes did then. Freddie Hart's "Easy Loving" was the number one country song on the radio and jukeboxes. I was working as a roustabout on a drilling platform about a hundred miles out of Morgan City, Louisiana. The weather reports were getting worse and rumors were flying that we would evacuate the rig within the next twenty-four hours. The air fairly crackled with suppressed excitement. The older hands kept calm, but I couldn't hold back a sense of foreboding and impending adventure as Camille tracked back and forth across the Gulf of Mexico like a woman who couldn't make up her mind.

It was a Wednesday, not that the day made any difference where all days are the same. We had finished our shift (called a tour, but pronounced like *tower* in oilfield lingo), cleaned up, eaten, and gone to bed a little after ten. We were suddenly awakened about midnight by shouts in the hall and loud banging on the door. It was one of the galley hands.

"Get up! Everybody up! We're evacuating!"

We worked all night tying down the rig. Up on the drill floor the roughnecks were coming out of the hole, uncoupling two miles or so of drill pipe, which we picked and stacked with the crane. With heavy chains and cable slings, we tied down everything that might move and a lot of heavy iron you wouldn't think a hundred mile an hour blow could budge. Daylight came with sullen red skies and foam-streaked seas. The men bitched and grumbled when they learned we were to evacuate by boat rather than helicopter, but I was secretly elated. The ride back to the shore would take us nearly ten hours.

Sometime around eight o'clock, the order finally came to evacuate. The crane operator began lowering us down, four at a time in the personnel carrier, onto the pitching deck of the supply boat. The tool pusher and the company man came down last, followed a few minutes later by the crane operator, who had to swing aboard on a line, a dangerous undertaking in bad weather.

The seas kept building as we pointed north towards Morgan City. Sheets of rain hissed across the water while the first guy started puking before we were out of sight of the rig, a big hulk of a roughneck rendered weak as a baby. This brought on a chain reaction and soon half a dozen men were groaning and retching, staggering toward the head, and not all of them making it. You would never guess to look at them, but many of the offshore hands were not at home on the water. Coming from small towns and rural areas of Texas, Louisiana, and Mississippi, they were fearless of heights and dangerous machinery, not to mention the constant threat of blowouts and sudden death by fire or explosion. But put them on a boat in rough seas and they became helpless.

Not that I never got seasick. Even Johnny Howard would head for the rail from time to time. Seasickness is the great equalizer, but I was lucky this time. There were more of us on board than available seats, but I managed to find a space in a corner where I could lay down and sleep for a few hours with a life jacket as a pillow. We reached calmer inshore waters in late afternoon and the men began to feel better and talked amongst themselves. We tied up at the dock outside of Morgan City a little after dark. Sprinting across the parking lot in a driving rain, I started the car and edged out onto the two-lane highway headed west. I bought a half-pint of whiskey at the first place I came to. That was a great thing about Louisiana: You didn't have to hunt for a liquor store. You could get a jug anywhere. At the same place, I bought a large coffee to go and sloshed some bourbon in before moving on.

Feeling a warm buzz of caffeine and alcohol, I headed for Texas, racing the storm. I kept the radio on for news bulletins. Camille was still on her way, though no one could be sure where she might land. We might have been headed straight on a collision course, for all I knew. There was nothing to do but try and make it to Houston. The towns and cane fields of South Louisiana went by in a blur to the beat of thudding wipers. There was plenty of traffic leaving Cameron and Intracoastal City, headed for higher ground.

After stopping for another large coffee to go, I topped it off with whiskey and drove on, turning onto I-10 at Lafayette. I kept the speedometer at fifty, the green exit signs going by in the rain. There wasn't enough visibility to go faster. Hurricane updates kept coming on the air every few minutes, advising everyone to evacuate low-lying areas. Occasional gusts of wind shook the car and the rain rattled on the roof. I made it as far as Orange just past the Texas line before pulling over at a Holiday Inn, where I registered and made straight for my room and a long hot shower. Outside, I-10 stretched on to Houston and beyond: to San Antonio, Kerrville, El Paso, and all the way to Los Angeles. But I was done for, hurricane or no.

Emerging from the shower, clean with the steam rising off my skin, I took stock, glancing around the room. I noticed a Magic Fingers massage box next to the bed where you could deposit coins. I remembered I had a joint I'd been saving and still had a couple of inches left in the half-pint. I took a sip and turned on the television. It was close to midnight, nearly twenty-four hours since we'd been rousted out of bed. I went through the channels full of snow and static, finding nothing on the air but a Billy Graham crusade. The camera showed a great many people in a big auditorium. There was organ music and preaching going on.

Feeding some quarters into the Magic Fingers box, I lit the joint and lay back on the bed, which was vibrating pleasantly. It was this, along with my fatigue and the last drink of bourbon, which made me aware of—or perhaps even caused—my rising tumescence. And so, as Billy Graham's Christian soldiers marched forward to be saved, as Hurricane Camille churned toward the coast, I found easy loving in my hand, giving myself up to the sweet dreams of my wasted youth.

Born Again

I don't understand what irks me about those smarmy television evangelists and their hideous, big-haired women. So-called Christians like Jerry Falwell and his ilk selling holy oil, swindling old ladies out of their money, talking about how herpes and AIDS are God's way of punishing sin. Billy Graham really is a saint compared to those people. I suppose what galls me the most is their assumption that they alone are the keepers of the truth. But enough of that.

For my part, I was lucky to be born again one afternoon on the Mescalero Apache reservation down in southern New Mexico. We had been three days working to put out a huge forest fire covering thousands of acres, with men flown in from all over the country to fight the blaze. I was separated from the others and was wandering alone when a vision came upon me. The experience was luminous. It was transcendent. It was ultimately indescribable. If I did not entirely grasp what was happening at the time, perhaps it was not the nature of my religion to reveal itself all at once. As I see it now, an old spirit set me loose upon the world with renewed faith in my life and purpose. Maybe one day I'll go back there and see if I might stay awhile and watch the game; maybe someone will come forward to explain the valley of the horse-skeletons, what might come in to a man there and mark him forever.

It was later that evening, about nine or ten o'clock, when we stopped for the bear cup. Since dark we had been holed up in a one-room schoolhouse waiting for our ride back to camp. As we wound through the blackened hills, the other members of the Pecos Eagles, our fire-fighting team, began talking softly. They stayed bunched up together the three days we had been on the fire. They were uneasy, bristling and muttering among themselves whenever we came upon a group of Indians on the trail. The Indians, some of whom had come from as far away as Alaska, laughed loudly, as if at some joke.

"*Hijo*, man I was glad to get out of there."

"Fucking *Indios*."

The fire was under control now, though some patches of flame still lingered up on the charred slopes. Abruptly, the driver stopped and set the brake. Leaving the motor running, he got down from the truck.

"*Que pasa?*"

"Look man, he's got a bear."

"*Mentiras*, that's bullshit, man."

"No, I ain't lying. *Mira*, he's got it."

The driver climbed back with the bear, which was tiny, singed, and whimpering. He wrapped it in a jacket and set it down by his feet. He drove us on to camp where, bone-weary, we crawled into our sleeping bags, the night turning colder, the stars reeling overhead.

I received my totem dream two or three days later, back home in San Miguel. In my dream, I became a bear that was nurturing, giving suck to the world. Lucky for me, I thought later, I never killed one. Now I knew I never would. The bear cub the driver picked up survived and was later taken to the zoo in Washington, D.C. It became a replacement to the original, aging Smokey the Bear.

So, what did I learn from my experience? It came in the form of marching orders. Follow the path. It was a vindication, a confirmation. I had long before made up my mind to live by my own dreams and to spend as little time as possible in the service of someone else's plan. Apart from the women I loved, I had two ongoing obsessions: music and a life at sea. My freshman year in college I went up to New York one weekend where I saw Carolyn Hester playing a club in Greenwich Village and I said, "Yeah, I want to play guitar and sing and have a girlfriend like that. We could make music and travel the world together."

Strangely enough, my dreams came true. All the ones that mattered. I like to think that old Indian spirit chose to come along to share my adventures and look after me occasionally. And I think it was he who gave me the nudge, the courage to get up and play and sing before an audience. This was my confirmation and warrior mandate. As for the bear, he . . . she . . . still comes to me in dreams. The bear, that most ancient and powerful of archetypes.

Music City

I left New Mexico in September 1971, returning to the Gulf Coast where I worked offshore out of Morgan City, Louisiana. We were working seven-seven then. It was during my off days in Houston that I started recording my first song demos. I also brought a new D-18 Martin guitar to replace a Gibson I had lost. According to plan, I moved to Nashville in June of 1972 after stopping off at the first Kerrville Folk Festival, which was not at all on the way, but made perfect sense in ways yet to be revealed.

It was in Nashville that I fell in with a hard-living group of songwriters and musicians: Guy Clark and his wife, Susanna, who had already been there a year or so, Rodney Crowell, Skinny Dennis Sanchez, and the looniest and most gifted of the bunch, Townes Van Zandt. Mickey White and Rex Bell came later, as did Steve Earle, the youngest of the group. Songwriting was not so much a business as it was a way of life. We lived it wide open, hammer down at full throttle, and the songs just came on their own.

After a few weeks in a boarding house on West End Avenue, I moved into a rented house on Acklen Street near Hillsboro Village. My first roommate moved out about the time Skinny Dennis moved in. Dennis played upright bass. He was tall, I think over six-five if you unrolled him all the way and stood him up straight. He had been staying with Guy and Susanna but moved in with us after he pissed Guy off by showing his ass real bad at a Fourth of July party, drunk on moonshine. Tall and dark-haired—taciturn to the point of severity—Guy was never one to suffer fools, gladly or otherwise. I believe he was happy when Dennis moved out. By then I found a job bartending at Bishop's American Pub on West End. There was a music scene going on there at night. Performers could pass the hat or drink three free beers. Bishop's became the first of what came to be known as *Writers' Nights* in Nashville. When the bar closed, we could come back to the Acklen house to party and play songs into the early hours.

In September, I drove back to Austin with Townes and a striking woman named Gloria, a publicist from New York who was madly in love with him. Townes had acquired a fiddle and was trying to learn to play "Farewell Tiawatha" the whole way. Badly. Townes was an accomplished guitarist, especially picking Lightning Hopkins-style blues. His fiddling was painful to the ears, but he was clearly enjoying himself. Gloria was not so amused.

"My god, Townes *please*. I can't hear myself think."

"Wait, listen to this," Townes resumed his screeching.

Once in Austin, we all ended up sleeping on the floor at a friend's house. Furious because Townes wouldn't get them a room, Gloria took a cab to the airport the next morning and flew back to Nashville. I don't recall if Townes had a gig that night or what happened in the days immediately following. I know we were all back in Nashville the next month for a concert at Peabody University with Townes, Guy, and a Texas band called Rat Creek. I played a guest set with Skinny Dennis accompanying me. That was the first time I ever played in a concert situation.

In November I went up to visit an old girlfriend in Cincinnati. I was horny and hoping to get some relief. Even though none was forthcoming, I wrote a song up there called "Piece of Wood and Steel" about my Martin guitar. This was later recorded by David Allan Coe on his second Columbia album, and was my first song to be covered by a major artist.

In December I rode the Greyhound to Washington, D.C. for

family Christmas at my sister's house. I could have driven but I was not averse to long bus rides then—I enjoyed them as an opportunity to eavesdrop on conversations and imagine the lives of the passengers around me. It was snowing lightly when my brother-in-law met me at the station, and snowing again a week or so later when I took a cab back from the Nashville station to our place on Acklen Street. By that time, Rodney Crowell and Mickey White had moved in. It was through Rodney that I met Mary, soon to become my second wife. Mary, the one who broke my heart.

A cold winter had set in by the time I moved out to share rent at Gloria's place, a carriage house behind an antebellum mansion near Hendersonville. This was early in the new year, after Rodney had found a place of his own. Dennis and Mickey weren't exactly the most responsible types when it came to rent and I didn't care to be responsible for collecting it. I felt like I was making as step up in the world as the Acklen house was becoming something of a crash pad. Gloria's place was far nicer and, moreover, she had a fabulous record collection. Though she was aggressive and bossy in a New York sort of way, I liked her. She had pale skin and raven hair pulled back tight like a matador. She wore hoop earrings and tight jeans tucked into black leather boots. She might have saved me from falling into the marriage trap, but she had eyes only for Townes. Then one cold night I built a fire for her in her upstairs bedroom. We talked for a while as one thing led to another, and later we made love while the flames cast dancing shadows on the walls.

Gloria and I sat at the table over coffee the next morning.

"You're not so bad," she said.

"Is that what you'd call damning with faint praise?"

"No, I mean it."

"You're not so bad yourself."

"Thanks."

"Well, I mean it too." But even as we sat there I knew—and she knew I knew—who she really wanted. And if she couldn't have

Townes, she had other irons in the fire. I was browsing through her LPs one afternoon when the phone rang. There came a significant pause when I answered.

"Is Gloria there?"

"She's out right now. Can I take a message?"

"Yes, tell her Chuck called."

At least I thought Chuck was the name he gave. "Okay, Chuck. I'll tell her you called."

"Chet," hissed the voice on the other end. "The name is Chet." I put down the phone, realizing my mistake. Chuck was not Chuck at all. Chuck was Mr. Guitar, head of RCA Records, one of the most powerful people in Nashville, or anywhere, in country music. Chet Atkins.

Although she had other boyfriends, Gloria had only one love besides Townes, and that was her German shepherd, Rover. In fact, the extreme fondness she showed to this dog belied her tough persona. I think I wanted to demonstrate my independence and show her I could find a woman on my own.

Mary was not yet twenty. She had long brown hair and sky blue eyes. A native Nashvillian, she had dated Rodney for a while. She was living with her mother when I invited her out to the country. Townes was in from the road and the four of us stayed up with a fire, listening to music. Snow fell all that night and on into the next day. That afternoon, Townes followed us in my old Volvo back into town while I drove Mary's Plymouth Duster. It was treacherous driving but somehow we made it, passing a lot of wrecked and abandoned cars on the way. I took this to be a sure sign our love was on the right track.

The whole city was shut down as Townes and I drove back.

"Man, thanks a lot."

"It's nothing."

"You know, I think I'm falling in love."

"She's a pretty girl," Townes was silent for a moment. "Hey, let's go see if we can find a drink."

"I don't know. It's still pretty slick out here. You know there's a jug back at Gloria's."

"Yeah, I guess you're right."

I found a job the next week framing houses. Townes had gone back out on the road. I didn't mind working all day, taking a quick shower, then driving into Nashville to play at Bishop's and see Mary for a couple of hours before driving back. You can do that kind of thing when you're in love. We decided to get married and set a date for the following month.

Back at the carriage house, Gloria and I often sat over coffee where the subject inevitably turned to Townes. "Do you think I'm important to him?"

"I know you are."

"I mean, I know how he is."

"He talks about you."

One of Gloria's endearing features was a tiny line of perspiration that sometimes appeared on her upper lip. "I don't really mind if I'm not the only one. I just want to be important."

"I'm sure you're important to him. He likes you a lot. He's just a little crazy, you know."

But I didn't really know. Townes always called her Sweet Pea. I didn't see much of Gloria after I moved out the following month. Mary and I had found a little efficiency apartment back in town, across the street from Bishop's Pub. We were married March 17th at her mother's house in Nashville. My parents flew in from Texas and sprang for a big rehearsal dinner. Skinny Dennis was my best man and I believe he was far more nervous than I was. We had a preacher and all the trimmings. Mary was stunningly lovely. Guy and Susanna had a party for us at their cabin out on Old Hickory Lake. When it was over, we returned to our new place and began married life together.

I worked into the summer with the framing crew, then quit one day after I thought I was going to get a song cut. Skinny Dennis and I had been making some demos over at Vector Music, which was run by a fellow named Harry Warner, who also happened to manage Jerry Reed. We had just finished putting down a song called "Close But No Cigar," a talking blues, when he happened by.

Jerry Reed had recently had a hit song called "When You're Hot You're Hot (When You're Not You're Not)." He was a hyperactive ball of energy bounding around the studio.

"Man, I really dig that song."

"Thanks."

"I'm not kidding. I want to cut that song."

On Monday, I showed up late at the site while the rest of the crew looked at me, waiting to see what kind of story I was going to come up with. "Well boys, I'm dragging up."

"You're leaving?"

"Yeah, Jerry Reed is cutting one of my songs."

The guys wished me luck and I said goodbye. But by the following week, I had taken a job working for J.T. Benson, a Christian book and record company. It seemed Jerry Reed wasn't going to record my song after all. Even if he did, we would still need money. Rex used to come over in the morning while I was drinking coffee after he had been up all night playing pinball. This was very early since at J.T. Benson, we started at seven o'clock, working four ten-hour days instead of five shorter ones. We used to listen to the radio while we packed up orders of records and hymnals. Willie Nelson was beginning to get airplay. A big hit song was Charlie Rich singing "Behind Closed Doors." J.T. Benson was a family-owned business and the employees were encouraged to believe we were doing the Lord's work, saving our souls while making them rich. There was always morning prayer: "Dear Jesus, we thank you for the nice weekend. Now let's get those orders out!" In the afternoon, I would crack a window up on the fourth floor and sneak a smoke behind stacks of records, thinking, "Dear Jesus, get me out of here!" I didn't last more than a few weeks at J.T. Benson.

I took a lot of jobs over the next few months, including remodeling, painting, and temporary manpower work. In early fall, I went to work out on River Road, remodeling a barn for a fellow named Roger Saloom. I was installing insulation one drizzly afternoon when I heard barking coming from across the road.

Looking up, I saw a spike buck angle down the hill and jump out on the rain-slicked road. With his mind on the dogs behind him, he never saw the car coming. He was already dead when I went down to help the fellow push his car back on the road. "I guess I'll have to report this," he said, looking at his damaged fender.

"Well, listen. You don't mind if I take this deer, do you? There's no use in letting the meat go to waste."

"No problem. I'll tell them it happened in the next county."

I dragged the deer up the hill and dressed it out. Mary and I ate a lot of venison chili that fall, with Skinny Dennis a frequent dinner guest. We had moved from our apartment to a duplex in Green Hills. Later, we moved to a cottage on some property in what was then the country, a few miles out Hillsboro Road. After an initial run of luck, I seemed to be going nowhere with my music and fell into depression. I made a bad mistake about this time and sold my Volvo, a good-running car that still had plenty of miles left in it. I had to depend on Mary for transportation and she resented it. She began to resist my advances and I began to suspect she was seeing someone at work. Through the summer and into the fall of 1974, we endured several separations. Then in December, Townes invited me to join him and Rex and Mickey for a Rocky Mountain tour, and I didn't hesitate to respond.

The Boys

It was a warm, overcast morning on the last day of December when I left Houston and flew up to Denver on the first leg of my trip up to Jackson Hole. I ran into Mary Dailey at the airport, Rex's Mary, who had come up on another flight.

"Hey, fancy meeting you here. Are you going up to Jackson?"

"Rex invited me to join him."

"All right, sounds like a party. Let's go get a drink. We've got plenty of time."

We had an hour's wait before boarding our flight on a two-engine prop plane that took us out of Denver, with snow-covered canyons and peaks spread out beneath us. After a while, the snow gave out as we passed over the high plains country, a sere, wintry brown. Snow appeared again as we crossed over the foothills of the Gros Ventres range. We made a quick descent, dipping sharply around a mountain and gliding down the Jackson Hole's single air strip. The stewardess thanked us as we taxied up to the terminal, adding as by afterthought: "Ladies and Gentlemen, it is bitterly cold today in Jackson Hole, with a ground temperature of twenty below zero."

Mary and I exchanged glances. "Holy cow, it was eighty this morning in Houston."

"Did you bring plenty of warm clothes?"

"I brought a ski parka."

"I've got a down jacket and long johns. I've even got felt boots from when I lived up in Michigan." I was glad I had come prepared, a thought that would return to me in the days to come. Out the window I could see Rex and Mickey jumping up and down and waving, with the Blue Unit, JJ's motor home, parked in the background.

Later, parked behind the Mangy Moose Lodge at Teton Village, we gathered around the captain's table in the back of the Unit. We were drinking whiskey chased with Coke. Townes, his new girlfriend Cindy, Rex and Mary, Mickey, and JJ. Rex was holding forth on the subject of footwear. "Shit boys, I came up here with my Texas City street punk shoes and skinned both elbows the first day falling on the ice." He wore an old green stocking cap, his ginger-red hair springing out around it. "If another skier had laughed at me, I'd have wrapped a goddamn ski pole around his ignorant head." Rex paused to take a snort of Dristan. "Ah, but I feel more like a skier since I found these shoes that make little tracks in the snow."

"You make tracks with your butt, too." Sarcastic to the max, JJ, a.k.a. Jimmy Joe Wanker, was never out of character.

"Well, listhen! You don't have to talk to me like that," Rex lisped, affecting outrage. Accompanied by a limp-wristed gesture of dismissal, a gay affectation, not an indication of his true nature, which was satiric. "Hmm." Rex's attention wandered to some girls passing outside the frosted window. "Dumplings. I mean we're surrounded by dumplings. I feel like a piece of chicken."

Townes took the bottle from JJ. "Following Rex's tracks is far out."

"Well, listhen!"

Outside, the long afternoon shadows angled across the snow as the sun dropped behind the jagged ring of the Tetons. It was two or three hours until show time. The bottle went around. Mickey White gazed disconsolately out the window. "What a bummer. All the girls up here already have boyfriends."

JJ reached for the bottle. "Yeah, skiers. You should give them up."

"Yeah, and they go for it right after skiing. They're blitzed by the time we hit the stage."

Townes gave Mickey a disgusted look. "They don't go for anything."

"Yeah, they do."

"I've sat next to Skinny Dennis at Fridays and I know what 'going for it' means," Townes appeared to pause in mid-thought. "But everything's real nice here, you know. We just have to iron out a few problems like freezing and starving to death. Little things."

During lapses in conversation, you could sense the cold. An unseen menace lurking just beyond the door, while inside ice rimmed the windows. The small butane heater kept up a steady roaring, but everyone kept their coats on.

"You know it's hard to be smart when you're such a dumb ass," Rex reached for his Dristan.

JJ said, "I'm so hip, Rex."

"Well, I tried to make an intelligent statement the other day."

"That was your first mistake."

Mickey took his guitar out and began tuning. "I'm gonna play 'Long Black Veil' tonight."

"Can I screw . . . uh, sing harmony?" Rex asked.

JJ: "Where the fuck's a glass? Somebody threw out all the glasses. Far out!"

Townes: "I figure the more coats and blankets the better."

JJ said to Cindy, a tall, sultry red head who had just turned seventeen, "Look dummy, this is a cup, right? All we need is a little Coke."

"You're treating me like a kid again," Cindy shot him a dirty look.

Rex searched through his pockets for his Dristan. "What time is it?"

JJ: "Too late."

"Let's not get too drunk tonight, boys, okay?" Townes' admonition was met with laughter and loose talk.

Rex: "What's cheaper would be to put baggies on each foot. Mmm, I've got on so much Chapstick my breath can't get past my lips. So I'm dumb, what am I supposed to do, kill myself? Shit, blow it off."

JJ: "Blow it off."

Mickey flat-picked some fast runs and rechecked his tuning. "Hey Townes. I think we should make it real show-bizzy tonight."

Townes grinned wolfishly. "Okay boys, we're going to make it real show-bizzy tonight. I've got on my show-bizzy shirt."

"No, I mean we should use all our good lines."

"Can't fool Mick." Rex took another snort of Dristan. Outside, the lights of Teton Village were shining through the ice-encrusted windows of the Blue Unit. Mickey and Rex began a forgotten argument. Townes took out his guitar and started warming up.

> *If I had a dollar bill*
> *Yes I believe I surely will*
> *Go to town and drink my fill*
> *Early in the morning*

He gestured rhetorically, "Ain't we a jolly crew?"

My notes, twenty-plus years old and counting, don't mention the first set that night. I know I came back to the Blue Unit early along with Cindy and a couple of guys to smoke a joint. When the rest of the crew came back, I pressed the record button on a small cassette recorder I had brought along. I transcribed only a few of these tapes I took on the tour, most of which were later lost in a fire that destroyed my parents' home in Houston.

Mickey: "I've never been so disgusted in all my life."

Rex: "I haven't. Those guys sitting up front talking about skiing. The louder we sing, the louder they talk. I heard somebody clapping."

Mary: "That was up in the balcony."

Mickey: "Hey, it's about midnight, you all."

Rex: "Can't fool Mickey."

Mary: "According to my watch, it's about four minutes to New Year's."

Mickey: "According to the clock outside, we've got ten minutes."
JJ: "Who cares?"
Mary: "I thought Wyoming was supposed to be wild. This place is pretty dead."
Townes: "Back in Jackson, the Cowboy Bar would be exploding right now. Here, it's just skiers. You know, middle class professionals. Not too wild."
Mickey: "I don't know. I bet there's people who like to get off."
Rex: "I want to get on, know what I mean?"
Mickey: "Anybody here got a cigarette?"
Mary: "Happy Birthday, 1975!"
Mickey, singing: "Good evening, friends."
JJ: "Up your ass."
Townes: "If I had a Harley 750, I'd ride it to Houston."
Mickey: "Happy New Year! Yahoo!"
Rex: "Well, just because a clock reaches a certain number, I'm not gonna jump up and down. 'Course, I could blow the spirit out of things real easy."
Townes turned to Cindy, his voice full of menace: "When I'm playing, you don't be with no other guys whatsoever. You either be watching me or be backstage. Don't be coming out here with two guys you've never seen before."
Rex says to Mary: "Yeah, make that a double."
Mary: "Kiss my ass. You don't listen to Townes and then tell me what to do."
Mickey: "Let's have a drink, boys."
Mary: "1975, far out."
Rex: "Anybody seen my green hat?"
JJ: "Your gangrene hat?"
Mickey, groaning: "Do we have to go up there again?"
Townes: "Yup, I'm gonna do her good, jukebox deluxe, if she stays like that. There's no sense in laying your ego on the line alongside your art. Unless you want it to get trampled. It's like laying your dick on a railroad track."
Rex: "I'm going to get me some mirror sunshades like Mary's.

Then for the rest of our lives we won't see each other."

Mickey: "Come on, boys, we need to go on right now."

I didn't make it back to the club for the last set. I had plenty of time, I figured. Owing to a combination of drinks, fatigue, and the sudden change in altitude and climate, I lay down on one of the bunks. I got up later when everyone trooped back in.

Townes, peering into his glass: "I think I have a hair in my whiskey."

JJ: "You eat out of the same bowl as a dog and you're worrying about a hair in your whiskey."

Rex: "Like picking a rig out of a trash can."

"True, that's true," mused Townes, still staring into his glass.

JJ: "Actually, you were drinking whiskey out of a dog's bowl. That was the night we were throwing darts. Far out party."

Rex: "Mary is getting Indian-drunk. She's got whiskey in one hand and chaser in the other."

New Year's Day

I was the first one up January 1, 1975, stepping outside for a pee just as the sun came up. There was a toilet inside reserved for emergencies, which this was not. The Blue Unit was in shambles, with coats, boots, and sweaters piled everywhere. A stale effluvia of whiskey, cigarette butts, and flat Cokes permeated the air. I could hear sounds of snoring and the gas heater blowing steadily, barely holding its own with the cold seeping through the walls. I walked over and got a cup of coffee at the lodge where the skiers were already up and clomping around in their boots, ready for a go at the mountain. Back at the Unit, I read for an hour or so before anybody started stirring.

About eleven, Rex went out, returning a few minutes later with a pint from the package store. I had a new tape in my recorder and pressed the button when he came through the door. "Boy, the sun is really out there."

JJ: "The sun is definitely out there."

Townes: "About ninety-three miles, a hundred and ten from Dallas."

Mary: "What are you talking about?"

Rex: "The sun, far out, huh."

And it was, shining hard and brilliant against the snow, straight out of a cold, blue infinity.

Mary, reading a flier: "It says here that Townes is 'a young, legendary Texas folksinger carrying on in the Jerry Jeff Walker tradition.'"

JJ, with a snort of derision: "I can spot one of those."

Rex: "I'll drink to that."

JJ with a non sequitur: "The way I figure it, I like war. It helps with population problems, keeps drunks off the road, and there are more women around. I think Vietnam was a good deal."

Mickey, bursting through the door: "Hey you guys, I made a deal with this guy to trade ski lessons for guitar lessons."

Townes: "I was playing this outdoor concert on the steps of the main library in New York City when this wino came up in the middle of a song. I took a swig out of his bottle, flipped everybody out."

Mickey worried that there were now more people eating in the lodge restaurant than were provided for in the contract. "Well, who wants to eat tonight besides me?"

Townes: "You get to eat every night, is that it?"

Rex: "I'm easy. I can eat any night."

Townes: "I can blow off goulash in a second."

Rex, lisping: "Well, listhen, how 'bout some sea food? Want some trouser trout? Limp ling?"

Through the glazed ice on the back window we could just make out some skiers attempting to play Frisbee with a garbage can lid. Rex rummaged around the overhead compartments until he found a real one and went out to join them.

"Anybody want to watch the Rose Bowl?" Finding no takers, Mickey slammed the door and headed off to the Moose to watch football on TV.

Townes: "Poor Mickey, he worries so much about us. He spends a lot of time here and he wants us to like this place, but I'm starting to like this gig. If I don't show it, it makes no difference."

Rex, storming back into the unit: "Can't play Frisbee in this atmosphere. I'd get out of breath just reading a book."

The bottle went round and round. When it was gone, another appeared. Townes told a story about Roger Miller. Then he invented a game. "Here's what let's do," he said. "Let's have a vote to decide who's the nicest and most considerate person among us."

Rex: "I suppose you would like to get yourself elected?"
Townes: "Just for fun."

A mock election was held. Townes won by one vote. "My mother always knew I had it in me," he said. "She always knew I had it on me, too."

The shadows grew longer, angling across the frozen parking lot. A pale sun went down behind a ring of mountains. The cold closed in. The first white men to come to Jackson Hole were trappers who used to sleep rolled up in buffalo robes in the snow. I couldn't see how they managed.

Cindy: "Townes, you need to take your vitamins."

JJ banged through the door, stomping and blowing on his hands. "I fell down ten times coming up that hill. Damn, you can step in dog shit here and it doesn't even get between your toes."

Rex: "I feel like a three-dog night here; three-dog night and no tail. I'm like these roaches. I'd rather face a can of Raid than go outside. Hmm, what's this?"

Mary: "Stimudent."

Rex: "Little stimulators, huh? I've got one of those."

Mary: "It's a little too big, Rex."

Rex: "Shh, darling. I don't want to brag."

JJ: "Look, there goes a drunk Saint Bernard."

Rex, peering through the frozen window: "Listhen, would you like a bone?"

JJ: "Like dogs, do you?"

Rex: "Shh, she's with Townes."

Townes: "I skied down a big slide into a swimming pool in Miami once. I was with Chris Smither, a folksinger from Boston. It was four in the morning. I woke up naked with this naked girl pushing on one lung and Chris pushing on the other while the manager of the motel was kicking us out."

Rex: "I had to sell blood one time in Nashville, I was so broke. I went straight to a pay phone and said, 'My name is Rex Bell and you can't use my blood. I've had hepatitis twice. I'm sorry, but I needed the money.'"

Mickey: "Doug Kershaw upstaged me here last summer."

JJ: "Well, Leon Russell did the same thing to him at Willie Nelson's Fourth of July picnic."

Mickey: "Ha. He punched out Joni Mitchell."

Townes: "That's nothing. Webb Pierce decked a blind guy at a bar one time, cold-cocked him. Cost him a bunch of money."

There was more talk of blind guys. Doc Watson once said to Townes, "Boy, that whiskey will kill you."

Sometime after the first set, on break in the Unit behind the Mangy Moose, Rex was soliloquizing. "This girl asked me why I wear sun shades at night. I told her it was because I was a very weird person."

Townes: "I ain't going in there again. I've been mistreated. I've been abused."

JJ: "Where's the whiskey? Yuk, this is Scotch. Where's the Dirty Old Bird?"

Mickey: "No more DOB?"

Townes: "In this band, we sacrifice drums and poontang for whiskey."

Rex: "The last time we were in Austin, Mickey got so horny we gave him twenty dollars and pushed him into this massage parlor. He was much nicer after that."

Mickey, ignoring Rex: "Hey Townes, I think you should pull your folk bag on them."

Townes: "I've pulled everything on 'em but a .38."

Rex: "Over here in America we eat salad and cows and then we eat it. In Bangladesh, they just eat it."

Townes: "There's so much good in the worst of us and so much bad in the best of us; it doesn't behoove any of us to talk bad about the rest of us. Abraham Lincoln said that."

Mickey: "He's dead."

Townes: "He still said it."

Rex: "Still dead, that SOB is still dead. Godammit."

JJ: "I'm talking about *Real* Still, you ever been sprayed with *Real* Still? I'm talking about rigor mortis."

Townes: "What we need is a chair."
Mickey, taking the bait: "What for?"
Townes: "For rigor mortis to set in."

Day Tripping

The next day came up gin clear, giving way to blue forever. Sentinel spruce and aspen rose up on the slopes of the Tetons under a vast dome of sky. Again, I was the first one awake, though too late on this morning to pee unobserved. After a quick pit stop at the Mangy Moose, I walked over to the condo the club owner had agreed to let us use for a few days, a welcome relief from the cramped quarters of the Blue Unit. The sun was well up in the sky and there did not seem to be such a fearsome edge to the cold. It felt good to get away for a while and stretch my legs. I knocked on the door and Cindy answered. I followed her back inside where she was fixing oatmeal. I didn't see Townes around and presumed he was sleeping. Cindy was a tall redhead with lots of freckles and pouting lips. She asked if I would like a bowl.

"Sure would. Thanks."

"There's plenty."

Going through a stack of albums, I found a Mariachi record and put it on the turntable. Then I remembered that a friend had given me a hit of acid before I left Houston. "Here's something to take with you to the mountains," he had said. Now the mountains were all around, suggesting, as always the possibility of magic and strange adventure. I knew you could get the same energy from the mountains as from the sea. You could find what you needed from either. Perhaps you could get the same from the desert of the Midwestern plains. "Hey Cindy," I called from the record changer, "you want to split a hit of acid?"

"Sure," she shrugged.

"Maybe you better ask Townes."

"It's okay. He won't mind." I cut the little pieces of blotter paper into halves and gave one to Cindy. Townes was up soon after. Before I could feel any effects of the acid, we were all on our way to Jackson, headed for the music store to buy guitar strings. As we pulled onto the highway, the skiers looked like tiny flyspecks way up on the mountain. The air began to take on a glowing radiance as I came on to that roller coaster feeling: Hang on, here we go, freewheeling into the melting landscape.

Mickey: "Hey, sixteen degrees, boys. It's warming up."

Mary: "I know a doctor who gave himself a vasectomy."

Rex: "Really? I bet he got a crick in his neck."

Mary: "Yeah, he had to go to a chiropractor."

Cindy sat by herself, gazing out the window. Townes rode shotgun up from with JJ. I sensed my whole life leading up to a single epiphany—a burst of illumination. Rex made his way up to the front of the Unit, hunkering down in the aisle between JJ and Townes.

JJ: "Quit beating on the goddamn ashtray with your fork."

"Fork you, Jack." Rex made his way toward the back and rummaged around in one of the overhead cabinets. "I need some help."

I could feel myself opening to the light and the snow-clad ring of mountains that spread out over Wyoming. "Rex, what you need is some spiritual help."

"Where are the spirits, as a matter of fact? Exactly what I was looking for."

Mickey: "Let's all join hands and contact the whiskey."

Back at Teton Village, we parked once again behind the Mangy Moose. It was later afternoon when I walked back to the condo. As the sun descended, the light faded to a quiet glow, suffused with pulsing energy. The aspen trees were swaying in a slow dance, and I knew they were girls, sirens beckoning to me through the window. Feeling their strange, irresistible pull, I stood mesmerized until darkness closed in.

I was still feeling the acid when I played a guest set later that evening, my fingers crawling like worms when I looked at them. I shifted my focus to the audience, who had no way of knowing how funny they looked. I found I could turn my attention inward on the song and wrap myself around it while losing myself within: a nice feeling as the roller coaster ran down through successively smaller peaks and valleys, coming down as the night wore on.

Jackson Farewell

Rewinding back to those lost days—days as Rex would say "slipped into the nebulous," I can't help reflecting that memories, like tapes, can also get old and brittle. Mickey wrangled us some free lift tickets and rentals, so one day we all went skiing. Only Townes and Mickey and I had any experience, though we were nothing to look at. The rest was mayhem. Then things got ugly one night after Rex and Mickey lost thirty-five dollars in a poker game. Townes turned on them with scorn and fury, "You lost! You motherfuckers lost!"

Mickey thrust himself forward, "He was a lucky man. You should have seen it. He was a shitty card player!"

"You lost to a mark! He got your money and split and now you're telling me and Rex is telling me what a shitty card player he is. He won your money and you're putting him down. Man, I'll go with him anytime. He's spending it right now."

Rex: "We could win it back easy."

Robert Jonson was on the cassette player, the only tape we had, singing "Some joker got lucky—"

I was gaining some valuable stage experience, playing every night our last week at the Mangy Moose, sitting in with either Mickey, Rex, or sometimes both. A foot or two of fresh snow had accumulated and the skiers in the audience all seemed to be in a much better mood. By now we had run through all the Old Crow at the package store next to the bar. Mickey continued to worry how eight of us were going to survive on six meal tickets. Rex continued his monologues and JJ kept sniping at him. Townes continued to admonish Rex for his drinking, but didn't mind his own.

One night after hours we ran into a cocaine blizzard courtesy of a guy who claimed he had a sailboat down in Florida, which he used to go back and forth into Colombia. He broke out his stash after the bar closed down for the night.

The bartender, Dave, took a mirror down from the wall, and began to polish it with a bar towel. His practiced manner suggested that this was not his first time. "Hey, that stuff must be pretty good," he said, "considering the tiny little bit you laid out for us."

That night, I followed a waitress home to her cabin in the woods at three in the morning and thirty below, my brain singing with whiskey and cocaine. "Don't breathe through your mouth," she warned. "You'll freeze your lungs."

She moved swiftly across the frozen crust, breaking through without breaking stride. Then the snow rose up as I fell, the stars reeling above me. I remembered the Jack London story "To Build a Fire" where the greenhorn up in Alaska freezes to death after falling through the ice, and then I heard her voice as if from far away. "Come on. Get up. I'm not kidding. You can die out here."

We stumbled up to her cabin, lost in winter solitude. She got a bottle of brandy while I started a fire. The cold was all around us, a sinister agent of malignant intent. I've long forgotten her name. We crawled into bed where we never even made love. But we did manage to get warm.

Mickey and I went skiing the next afternoon and I felt a little more confident. Traversing along a narrow stretch of trail, I spotted a porcupine sleeping in an aspen tree. I could see where he had eaten all the bark around him. I waited for Mickey, who was coming up behind me, and pointed with my ski pole. "Hey Mick, look. It's a snow turkey."

"Oh yeah," he squinted through his glasses.

"Really. They're very rare."

Mickey continued to stare. You could fool him sometimes.

We skied out of the woods and turned, racing down the mountain. Mickey had allowed as how he could ski faster and—with my rediscovered confidence—I set out to challenge him. I got way out ahead of him, but missed a turn about three hundred yards from the bottom. I somersaulted out of both skis. Going up for the last run, feeling the chairlift steadily humming, I felt a thrill each time we bumped past a tower. I could feel the eternal brooding presence of the mountains. The ski resorts, the lodges, and condos had just been campsites. The Indians, buffalo, and mountain men had been there just the other day. I wanted to come back in a thousand years, live in a teepee, eat dog and venison, steal horses.

Back in the Blue Unit, Rex was holding forth. "I used to have a paper route. I had a motor scooter and rode in the parade in Houston with JFK. The next day he went up to Dallas and ate it. He also had a lot of hair. You know, I had a girlfriend once. She was so tall I had to go up on her . . ." Gazing through the frozen glass, Rex sang to the tune of an old Christmas carol, "Jack Frost nipping on a half a pint/Lying shitfaced in the snow . . ."

We left on Monday, January 14th, departing Jackson Hole in a snowstorm. Townes was sick with the flu, Mickey had a sprained shoulder from doing handsprings, and the rest of us were wheezing and sneezing. Dave the bartender gave us a parting gift of a handful of white crosses for the journey.

From Jackson we headed south on Highway 189, following the Snake River for a while then breaking into open, rolling country with sagebrush poking up through wind-sculpted snow drifts. The Blue Unit swayed along like a big cabin cruiser, red Christmas lights knocking against the window, and Robert Johnson on the cassette player. Rex and I ran in for a pint at Pinedale, where a weathered old timer gave us the once over. "That pint ain't gonna last you boys very long."

Rex agreed. "No sir, it's about like throwing a hamburger patty to a pack of wolves."

We drove on with the Wind River Range and the Continental

Divide off to our left. JJ chain-smoked Marlboros, sipping from a bourbon and Coke, and Townes rode shotgun with Cindy in his lap. The country opened up under vast galleries of sky, with high cirrus clouds in hues of pearl. We passed signs reading BIG SANDY RIVER, PETRIFIED WOOD BARN, and then a trailer camp for oil field workers. Townes talked about his father, dead ten years, an oilman like my own dad.

We stopped for another pint at the Paradise club in Eden where hay bales lay stacked against the long winter and jet trails scratched across the sky. A drilling rig was working off to our left out of the hole with all the pipe racked. I shivered involuntarily, thinking it must be a cold son of a bitch roughnecking out there. We passed a hawk on the highline, another working rig, and a herd of antelope not fifty yards off the road. Turning east on I-80 we put Rock Springs behind us, heading out across the Red Desert where a sign read WAMSUTTER 66, CHEYENNE 264. The sun dropped behind us. We passed another drilling rig. JJ, Townes, and I split the last of the white crosses. Johnny stopped once to try emptying the sewage tank, but it was frozen solid.

Townes then took the wheel. He was shirtless, lean and muscular, and full of scars. The twin stripes of the Interstate ran on across a vast emptiness as we crawled across the bottom of Wyoming. Mickey and Cindy were sleeping. Mary was loving on Rex. I passed the bottle over to Townes. "Lots of space out here."

"Yeah I know. I'm filling up half of it."

As the sun dropped down behind us we passed a long train of truck trailers riding piggyback, headed west. We made good time trundling along with a strong tail wind. We pulled over for a sunset piss-call, the slanting rays of sun silhouetted banks of cloud, setting off an explosion of radiance. Windblown ice crystals whipped across the road. Townes paused as we walked back to climb aboard: "Did you hear the song General Custer wrote just before the Battle of Little Big Horn?"

"No, what was that?"

Townes began singing to an old tune from *Porgy and Bess*.

"It ain't necessarily Sioux—"

Denver

Conventional wisdom has it that, barring an accidental overdose from heroin that's too pure, you can live a long time as a junkie. There are plenty of old drunks around, 'more old drunks than there are old doctors,' as in Willie Nelson's song. So maybe there are lots of old heroin users around too. I had never been tempted to try it, though I had been around it from time to time. I even held Townes off once, squeezing his arm to make his veins rise up.

Now, in Denver, there was a change in the air. If you didn't catch on immediately, a dead give-away was listening to JJ Wanker sniffing and scratching all night on the couch across from me.

The next day I was stretched out on the same couch that I had more or less chosen as my space. I was reading *Burr*, a novel by Gore Vidal. Townes and Cindy had sequestered themselves in the Blue Unit, as had Rex and Mary in the guest bedroom. JJ was gone somewhere, which suited me fine. I was two or three chapters into my book when Mickey hit me with a strange request, "Hey Ricardo, would you walk around the block with me?"

"Huh? Say what?"

"Man, I think I'm gonna nod out."

I looked at Mickey who seemed altogether too alert to be nodding out. "Go on Mickey. You look okay. You'll be fine." That was a hell of a way to treat a brother, but I didn't feel so much compassion. The Boys had not included me in their deal and I didn't feel like having anything to do with it now. I was surprised that Mickey didn't try to keep their drug shooting a secret like the rest, but as *Burr*—or perhaps it was Gore Vidal—said, "In the end all things are known, and few are important."

I was right about Mickey. He was okay. We had several days off in Denver. Most of the pay from the Mangy Moose had gone to advances and we were now all broke. Even Townes had to wire back to Austin for a loan. Understandably, our hosts, old friends from Houston, couldn't be expected to feed everybody. It happened that The Boys got sober and hungry pretty damn quick. Then Townes caught Mickey scooping cheese spread out of the jar with his finger. "Use a knife, you pitiful motherfucker."

"Fuck you, man!" Mickey swelled up displaying like a bantam rooster, whereupon Townes seized the jar of cheese spread and spit in it. Mickey spit back at Townes, taking care to miss.

The next day I received some Western Union money wired from my folks and treated myself to breakfast at a Pancake House. Later, Rex and I walked to the liquor store where we bought a pint. "I see you boys found some more pennies," and the lady behind the counter.

"Yes ma'am," said Rex, not in the least offended. Back at the house, the pint lasted for ten minutes of competitive drinking. I nearly made myself sick making sure I got my share.

Our next stop was the Oxford Hotel, a grand old place near the train station downtown with an atmosphere of decayed elegance and an Art Deco bar where I spent ten of my last twenty dollars. I was trying to hold on to my last ten but Rex and Mickey knew I had it on me and stuck to me like glue until I used it to buy a bottle. Later, sitting around in one of the rooms upstairs, JJ, Rex, and Mickey addressed themselves to an analysis of Cindy's personality.

Mickey: "I couldn't stand her for an hour."

JJ: "I'd kill her in an hour."

Rex: "I like her."

JJ: "What you've got is your basic seventeen-year-old with a twenty-one year-old body and the mind of an eight-year-old."

Rex: "There's nothing I'd like better than having a dumb

seventeen-year-old sucking my dick."

JJ: "Hey, outta sight!"

Mickey: "Yeah!"

We stayed two nights at the Oxford Hotel. On the second night Townes and the boys played a great first set. By the second set the room was half-empty and everyone was roaring. Townes sat hunkered off to one side of the stage while Rex and Mickey played half a dozen numbers. Then he stood, swaying slightly, and attempted to play "Farewell Tiawatha" on a fiddle someone had given him. I remembered our ride with Gloria to Austin. Townes was a mesmerizing performer when he put his mind to it, but his fiddling hadn't improved. Not a bit. Nervous titters passed through the audience while he commenced a mournful screeching. After a time, Townes set the instrument carefully on the stage, then standing, brought his boot smashing down upon it. That's a weird sound, a man stomping on a violin—kind of like a delivery truck running over a turtle. Townes picked up some pieces of the fiddle and tossed them out among the audience like party favors or Mardi Gras beads.

Moving On

Everyone was happy to be moving again when we left the next morning for Crested Butte, which was our next stop and penultimate gig of the tour. We'd scored a bag of weed and stopped for gas on the way out of town at a station with novelty items displayed in the window. Townes went in to pay the bill, returning with a stuffed dog, a giant cigarette lighter, and a butterfly net. At another stop he purchased a pair of sunglasses and a pint of Old Crow. We had one more stop to make—at the drugstore for some crab medicine for JJ, who claimed to have caught them sleeping in a bed where Rex had slept. Thus provisioned, we set off down the road again with Robert Johnson signing, "I got rambling, rambling on my mind . . ."

Rex, talking to no one in particular: "White Freight Liner, get it on, amigo."

Mickey: "There's a narc in a White Freight Liner."

Mary: "Oh my God."

"Shhh, get the pot off the dashboard." JJ pulled over to the shoulder. Robert Johnson was abruptly silenced. We all held our breath as the officer approached.

"I'd like to see your driver's license and proof of ownership." Palpable silence continued while the officer examined JJ's papers. "We've got designated lanes here."

"Is that the deal?" Whatever else, JJ Wanker was fearless in talking with the cops.

"Right, just keep on the right side."

"Okay, thanks, I didn't know." The highway patrolman walked back to his car while JJ eased back on the pavement, taking care to signal. Robert Johnson went back on and I turned my recorder on to what would prove to be the last tape I transcribed.

Mary: "What town is this?"

Townes: "Fairplay. Let's stop and get some liquor and butane."

Mickey: "Let's get a jug first and then get some butane."

JJ: "Hold it. I don't want to pull into a liquor store right after the cops stopped us."

Mickey: "Cops can kiss my rosy butt."

Rex: "That's cool. We can just tell him he shook us up and we needed a drink."

Mickey: "Fairplay, huh?"

JJ: "No shit."

Rex: "Think we might find a game here?"

JJ: "Okay, we're gonna park right here."

Mickey: "I want a cheeseburger and a Coke."

There followed a chorus of "me toos."

Townes, "Sure everybody gets to eat. We need seven cheeseburgers and seven Cokes. Go clean the window, Mick."

JJ: "Naw, he's too sensitive."

Townes: "What we need is a perfectionist for a window cleaner and you obviously ain't one."

"A far cry from per-fucking-fection," and Rex on his way out to clean the back window.

JJ, referring to Rex, "Look at that nigger."

Townes: "Hand me a towel and I'll hand it to Rex through the window. Hey man, get it once with the towel and it'll be perfect."

Rex returned, stomping and whistling, "Cold out there. I turned the towel around and it still looks messy."

Mary: "I smell gas."

Rex: "Hold it, the butane's off."

Townes: "Fix it or blow our ass to kingdom come."

Mary: "Anywhere in America you can get a cheeseburger."

Rex: "Not true, you can't get a cheeseburger at the bottom of Niagara Falls."

Townes: "Or the tip of the Tetons."

Rex: "Did you see Mickey take off his shades before he went in there to get the cheeseburgers?"

Townes: "Rex, the heater's smooth fucking off and blowing raw butane . . . going to blow us all to smithereens."

Rex: "I like this one-horse diner. It's like a three-stool taco stand in Tijuana. Ever seen one of those? I got trapped in one when I got burned for a blow job. I slammed the door and this cop said I busted it. I told him I didn't have any money but he didn't believe I was broke."

Mickey returned with a paper bag full of cheeseburgers and began passing them out. Everyone turned to food but Townes, who was reading horoscopes from a tabloid. "It says here 'Ex-coroner faces probe on embalming boy.'"

Rex: "I figure the boy faces the probe."

Mary: "You can't get embalmed unless your parents give you permission."

Townes: "Here's one: 'Oak Leaf, Kansas. Police tried to dispose of 139 pounds of marijuana by burning it in the courthouse incinerator. The police quickly put out the fire and removed disposal operations to the city dump after the courthouse began filling up with smoke from the weed.'"

Rex: "Goddamn."

JJ: "Who took my hamburger? Hey man, I wasn't through. That's a bummer, Mickey, stealing my food."

Mickey: "I had this irresistible urge. It's this disease I have."

Mary: "These are good. I'm talking about homegrown French fries."

JJ slipped into the driver's seat and cranked up the Unit. "Okay, here we go."

Rex: "Don't forget to stop at the liquor store."

Townes: "Mick, you go in. Just buy a pint, don't get a fifth."

"I just took my shoes off." Mickey went back out anyway.

Mary: "Light the butane, it gets cold back here."

Townes: "Hey, Rex."

"Yeah."

"Avoid involving yourself in matters of which you have no knowledge. You're a Leo, aren't you? Here's JJ's and Cindy's: 'Take care that your actions early in the day don't leave you open to those kinds of criticisms you find impossible to bear.'"

JJ: "Too late, huh?"

Rex: "I'm a Leo."

Mary: "You're a Virgo."

JJ: "Rex is alligator gar."

Rex: "I read one book says I'm one thing, another says I'm another. In the real nitty gritty I'm a Leo. I'm a Leo with a penis rising, and my moon is in my pants."

Mickey climbed back on board with the bottle in a paper sack. "Is that a French fry?"

Mary slapped Rex's hand, which had wandered to her breast. "Don't Rex!"

"Creep."

"That's why I got sore tits."

"Bullshit."

"How come since I got you to quit they quit being sore?"

"Punk. That was a week ago."

"Don't call me punk."

Mickey: "Who wants a hit of French fries before I eat the rest of these?"

Mary: "Let go of me."

We pulled out onto the road, picking up speed, headed for Gunnison and Crested Butte. The bottle went around. You could hear Robert Johnson above the whine of the tires.

Crested Butte

Townes ambled up to the stage, reached out, and tapped the microphone. "Ladies and gentlemen, on guitar tonight we have Mickey White. We call him Egg White because he's only been laid once. And over here on bass we have Rex Bell. We call him Gravity Bell because he never lets us up. And I'm Townes Van Zandt." Townes bowed with mock gravity to scattered applause and cat-calls.

Rolling back the tape, it seems strange we survived those days and nights. I must have kept my spirit guide busy looking after me. Maybe I let him down. Excess for its own sake had achieved a momentum all its own. I had come along for the ride, and now I had to ride the one I drew, a nightly test of physical and emotional endurance. Nobody endured like Townes, who was by turns droll, maudlin, lugubrious, gentle, caring, and vicious. He slept light. Sometimes late, towards the dawn hour, listening over muted snores, I could hear the faint sound as he unscrewed the bottle, followed by the chink and flare of his Zippo lighter, holding the night together while the others slumbered on.

"You doing all right?"

"Yeah."

It seemed that Townes suffered Rex and Mickey and the rest of us because he had grown tired of touring alone. He and Rex had gone out together a few years before on the college circuit but as far as I knew, he usually traveled solo. I'm not sure when the idea came to put the band together. Probably it was when JJ brought the Blue Unit.

The Boys had already been out to Chicago and back before I hooked up with them. JJ may have been a borderline sociopath, but he kept his act together when it came to driving. Once we were parked, it was Katy-bar-the-door. It was his habit to make a beeline straight to the mixing board to harass the sound man, and once there, to drive some poor devil to tears or apoplexy.

Meanwhile, Rex kept up his monologues on stage or off, his mind stripped down and customized like a hot rod, making a joy ride on our nightly rush to oblivion. Mickey had booked the tour. He was a whirling dervish. Strange people were drawn to Townes. He kept them around, I think, because they kept him amused. But he knew what it was like to be crazy. If he wasn't crazy to being with, thirteen months of shock treatment years before had put him over the edge.

Despite all the ongoing weirdness, there were nights when the magic shined through. Mickey and Rex knew Townes' moves, his phrasing and unpredictable tempo shifts. When Townes was on, he was great. When he was too gooned—or pretended he was—he often hunkered down on a corner of the stage, immobile, while he let Rex and Mickey play. I filled in from time to time. People who had never been around Townes were amazed. He had a way of bringing out extremes in people, of making them want to shed their inhibitions so they could be for a night maybe just a little bit like him.

Wherever we went, Townes' reputation preceded him, and we were met with fresh troops, ready to party. Crested Butte, an old mining town filled with rich hippies, ski bums, and shaggy bearded mountain men, was no exception. I got lucky the first night and found a place to hole up where I slept with—but again did not make love to—a woman named Ronda. Sometime during the night she flung her long john top to the floor, where it landed half in and half out of the cat box. In the morning she picked it up and put it right back on. A feral woman, Ronda had nice tits.

The weird got weirder that afternoon, ratcheting up the tension when Mickey slipped a steak knife into Spot, Townes' stuffed dog, leaving it from him to find. Townes became unglued, his face twisted in a mask of anguish. "Who killed Spot?"

For reasons equally inexplicable Rex stepped in and took the blame. "I did it, so what?"

"You stabbed my dog!"

"What's the big deal?"

"How could you kill Spot? You might as well put a knife in me."

"It's a stuffed dog. You're worried about a stuffed dog. That's absurd."

"You killed Spot," Townes' voice was breaking and real tears came. "You put a steak knife in Spot's heart."

Mickey kept silent. It was only later after the funeral with Spot interred in a snowbank that the truth came out, in the way that all things have a way of becoming known. Still, it was bad business to bring out the knives because JJ pulled one on Rex later that night. Townes stepped in between them at the last instant, grabbing JJ by the wrist.

I was happy to miss this action. Ronda let me hang out in her cabin another night. I was tired and broke again, and needed respite from the craziness. Ronda had a complete collection of Jimmie Rodgers records and I listened to them all before falling asleep on the couch. She came in at about four-thirty with a guy from New Mexico, still wearing her long john top from the night before. Several inches of snow and fallen, and it was still coming as I walked back in eerie quiet to the Blue Unit where all the bunks were full. I turned in on the floor close to the heater with my down jacket wrapped around me. A little while later Townes awoke and gave me a blanket.

One Long Day

A warm sun marked our mid-morning departure from Crested Butte, but snow began to fall as we wound our way up the road to Monarch Pass. Near the top it became a blizzard. Back at the captain's table Mary and Rex were trying to teach me a card game called Crazy Eights, but my attention kept wandering to the situation outside. I made my way to the front to peer out between JJ and Townes, only to find we were in a white-out a few hundred feet from the top of the pass.

"How's it look?"

Townes remained impassive, "Not looking good."

"Really," JJ squinted ahead. At that instant a palpable wave of fear swept through the Unit as through a herd of antelope catching scent of the lion, or a school of mullet scattering under the shadow of the pelican.

Mary: "We're gonna die!"

Rex: "Shut up."

Mickey: "Well, at least if we're gonna die it's gonna be in good humor."

JJ: "I don't know. I could feel pretty shitty."

Rex: "I can't see nothing."

JJ: "Neither can I."

With no way to tell what was road and what was not, or even what was up or down, the Blue Unit nosed into a snowbank and we shuddered to a stop. Townes, JJ, and I managed to open the door a little and squeeze out. Beyond the piled up snow the slope fell away into the abyss.

Townes: "What do you think?"

JJ: "Another foot and we'd have been goners."

Townes looked around, "Well, we've got butane so we won't freeze for a while. Lucky for the snowbank or we'd have gone straight over the cliff."

"I don't know, there might be a guard rail under all that snow." I walked toward the back just as lights approached out of the swirling gloom. It was a big yellow snowplow. I approached the driver, who leaned over to roll down his window. "Is the pass closed?"

"If it is, somebody's gonna get their tit caught in a wringer."

"Can you pull us out?"

"Yeah, there's a chain back there."

I was thankful that, for once, my years of oil field work had finally proven useful. I dragged the heavy chain and found a place to hook beneath the back of the Unit, then hooked the other end to the snowplow. The driver put it in gear and pulled the Blue Unit effortlessly from the bank. I returned the chain, looping it back where I found it and walked back up to thank the driver. "Do you want us to follow you down?"

"No, you go down first 'cause I'm going to be plowing six inches from the cliff."

"Okay, thanks man. You saved our butts."

The driver nodded curtly and put his machine into gear. We climbed aboard the Blue Unit. Rex placed a pair of dice on the dashboard face-up, showing seven, and we eased on up to the summit of Monarch Pass. We hadn't gone a quarter mile before the snowplow roared past, throwing a great glop of snow against the windshield.

JJ: "Damn."

Townes: "That's okay. I think we're gonna make it now."

But more trouble lay ahead. We were headed back north again, trying to make our last gig at the Pioneer Inn in Nederland, near Boulder. We had not reckoned that our way might be blocked.

A sign at the entrance to the Eisenhower Tunnel read: CHAINS OR SNOW TIRES ONLY. A highway patrol officer at the entrance motioned us to turn around. With darkness approaching we were down to half a quart of Ezra Brooks and $2.57 between the seven of us. Where, one might ask, did the money go? Was it all eaten up in advances and bar tabs?

JJ made a U-turn and we pulled off by the shoulder. "What are we going to do?"

Rex: "Let's sleep in the Unit and try again tomorrow."

Townes: "We're down to no money, no booze, no food, and if we run out of butane, we freeze to death."

Mickey's face lit up: "Wait a minute, you guys. I got an idea. This just might work. My cousin's ex-wife, she and her new husband have a motel in Breckenridge. Maybe they'll cash a check for us and put us up."

Rex: "Let's try it, we've got nothing to lose."

Mary: "I've got a check but I don't think I've got that much money in my account."

Mickey: "There's a phone booth. I'll see if I can reach them."

We sat in silence with the motor running. After a time Mickey came trudging back through the snow.

JJ: "He looks happy."

Mickey burst through the door. "All right boys, we're in luck! They have room and they'll cash a check for us."

A chorus of cheers broke out. "Yea Mickey! All right. Way to go!" JJ turned onto the icy pavement. In the back Rex and Mary resumed their game of Crazy Eights by candlelight. It was past dark when we rolled into Breckenridge and found the motel. Mickey and Mary went in to register, returning a few minutes later with the keys to two rooms. I followed Townes and JJ into one, anxious for a long, hot motel shower. When I came out they were romping about, jumping from bed to bed. An end table went over, along with a lamp and then the sound of splitting wood. A little later I found Mickey down at the bar. He was still on a roll, "Hey Ricardo, you want to play some songs for free drinks?

There's a PA set up and I've already cleared it with the bartender."

"You bet, let me go get my guitar."

Back at the Unit I found Rex and Mary. "Do you want to come pick a while?" I asked Rex.

"No way, we're gonna hang out here."

"Okay, see you later."

Back at the bar, Mickey already had the PA turned on and was ready to go. He brought a couple of beers up to the stage while I tuned. We played about thirty minutes before Townes showed up with a distressed look on his face. "Have you guys seen Cindy?"

"She's not in here."

"I can't find her anywhere."

After a time, I left Mickey at the bar and went back upstairs where I found Townes in a panic.

"Man, Cindy's gone."

"She's got to be around someplace."

"I'm telling you, she's gone!"

"Take it easy, she's got to be around."

Townes called his mother back in Houston. Then he called the sheriff and reported Cindy missing. He was weeping openly now, and I welled up with sympathy tears. After a time, a sheriff's car and deputies arrived, but not before the phone rang. It was Cindy, who had used her key to open the wrong room and had fallen asleep. Townes tried to explain the situation to the deputies, who looked at him with utter loathing and disgust.

I found Mickey back downstairs at the bar. "What's up?"

"Cindy's okay. She was sleeping in another room."

"That figures."

Our credit was good for another beer and I joined Mickey at the bar. There were only a few people in the room and we sat talking with the bartender, who was washing up glasses. Then Townes showed up a few minutes later, causing the bartender to lose his friendly demeanor. Townes was wrapped Indian-style in a blanket from the room. The bartender turned to Mickey, all the nice-guy gone out of his voice, "Get him out of here."

"Don't you know who that is? That's Townes Van Zandt. He's got seven records out."

"I don't give a damn who he is, I want Blanket Man out of here.

Texas Bound

You could tell the Boys were feeling homesick when talk turned to fishing. JJ brought out his tackle box and we looked over his bass lures. In Nederland, near Boulder, we were sitting round the captain's table, parked behind the Pioneer Inn. The conversation turned to saltwater: speckled trout and redfish, sharks and stingrays, camping by a driftwood fire, and flounder gigging on still evenings. Here we were, high in the Rocky Mountains where you could find fossilized shells from ancient sea beds, where a late afternoon sun slanted down on cars whizzing through the slush, where a school bus was unloading, and a dog angled across the street keeping an eye out for traffic, where a car full of pretty girls stopped at the light.

Another band played that night, but Townes and the Boys entertained anyway, doing handstands and cartwheels, fake fights and pratfalls. JJ did his trick of removing his cowboy boots while standing on his head. Mickey got down on the floor and did a barking seal imitation, a new one for me.

The next morning, bad vibes invaded the Unit, and plenty of them, over something that had gone down with Townes and Cindy.

"I'm gonna get another advance and fly your stupid ass home, dumpling."

Rex: "Smart's a bummer, let's all get dumber."

It was Townes who had asked us to quit calling Cindy stupid. A Texas State ranked champion in horse jumping competitions,

Cindy wasn't exactly stupid. She had only just turned seventeen and was running with a rough crowd. She liked to stay stoned and she talked only to Townes, ministering to him and hanging on with both arms around him, kind of like he was a horse. Now, hurt and brooding, she retreated into stony silence.

I was reading from a slender volume of Lao Tzu I had found, "Truthful words are not beautiful; beautiful words are not truthful." I wondered which was more important. And didn't Keats say: "Beauty is truth, truth beauty?" And how much did a Greek urn, anyway?

On Saturday night, I went home with a barmaid whose name was Maggie, a hell-raising, whiskey-drinking woman who fit right in. This time, and not merely for warmth, I got my ashes hauled good and proper. We spent Sunday afternoon shooting dice with Rex and Mary, a new game called Hog. That evening Townes and JJ huddled over road maps. We were headed home that night after the show. With the temperature rising to fifty degrees, it was the warmest day we had experienced in weeks, and it seemed a promise of what lay in store for us a thousand miles to the south.

That night, a huge guy with a beard and bib overalls laid some more acid on us. If you ever wondered where all the hippies had gone, you could still find them in the mountains. They were hustling to make a living, with jobs scarce and pay low. And there was the snow that lasted forever, slowly filling up with dog shit. Everybody had a dog up there, big ones. This was truth. And the mountains thrust up so massively you could feel them pulling as if you were magnetized. The air was so clear you wanted to reach out and touch them from twenty miles away. This was beauty.

The hills of Tennessee had their own beauty: lush with hot, green summers and pale winter skies, ranging blue to monochrome, where the mere mention of snow sent the locals into a panic. Where I wondered if David Allan Coe, the Mysterious Rhinestone Cowboy who had recently recorded one of my songs, was going to wind up becoming a star and sell a zillion records, making me comfortable, if not rich. Then I would be vindicated in my Mary's eyes. More than an agreeable fantasy, this was the way it was all supposed to happen. I might even start a band of my own and take it on the road. I was going to make it sooner or later, whatever making it meant. It was all just a matter of time. It mattered no more than ripples from a stone tossed into a pond. Which was all our passage through these mountains amounted to, though I liked to think they might bear some imprint, however infinitesimal.

We left Nederland and the Pioneer Inn with Maggie the barmaid, who heard the siren call of Texas and decided to come with us to Austin. She brought along her dog, named Dumpster, after the place where she had found him. Dumpster was a starved, pitiful creature Townes took to right away, a replacement, no doubt, for poor Spot, who lay buried in a snow bank back up the trail in Crested Butte.

Rex, Townes, and I each swallowed a hit of acid coming down Boulder Canyon. It began to take hold almost immediately in a way that suggested this was no mere recreational dose. We also had a full pint of whiskey and two cans of Orange Crush to wash it down. Sitting round the captain's table, we soon convulsed into giggles. Townes began to look more and more Indian. I once told my mother he was of Dutch origin, Van Zandt meaning "of the sand." "He's Black Dutch," I said without realizing that the term referred, not to skin or hair, but to the dark clothing worn by a religious sect.

"No, I think he's Indian," my mother had said. Maybe she was right. Townes was looking Indian now, his eyes glittering obsidian, an aura flashing rainbow colors like heat-lightning out on the plains. The lights and reflections from the road became myriad, spinning pin wheels with sparks, fire, and Roman candle star bursts in the night. Rex, the eternal joker, became a lurid, glowing clown.

It seemed to take ages to reach JJ up front at the wheel as the Blue Unit cruised south in the night toward Colorado Springs.

"Doing okay?"

"Oh yeah."

"Wow, lots of lights out there. This shit is really strong."

"Yeah, I know. I took two."

"Bullshit." I knew JJ was lying, but the thought was enough to send me on the long journey back to the captain's table.

Somewhere in the night we passed a wreck involving two cars and an eighteen-wheeler. One of the cars lay upside down. There were red smoking flares, the flashing lights of ambulance and Highway Patrol cruisers, a luminous blue and red swirling scene. It was a vision of death; of souls hovering in terror and confusion at being rent so suddenly from their bodies. A sucking intake of breath came from up front as JJ steered around the carnage. Mickey said, "Let's all be thankful, boys." Maggie, the mountain woman's Boston accent came back to her, "Oh my God, there's only half of that car."

Townes, Rex, and I ceased our giggling. Rex was now pulsating a bluish green. We were alive, and life itself was but a dance with death. While the mountains would only last a little longer, Mother Earth herself would one day burn to a cinder, as would the sun in its own time.

Now our last can of Orange Crush assumed great importance. We took polite, measured sips, careful to make it last. As it warmed up towards the bottom, it became Booger Crush. Booger Crush following a sip of whiskey. The wreck forgotten, we collapsed in gales of helpless laughter. At some point, Townes opened a window and threw out the rest of the acid. Somewhere near Trinidad, JJ pulled over at roadside rest area and we stumbled out to pee. We found ourselves on a high plateau with dawn streaking the sky.

Rex and I stood at the urinal where a sign on the wall read: CAUTION DO NOT DRINK THE WATER. "Man, am I reading that right? What does NON POTABLE mean?"

"It means booger, Rex. You can't drink it."

"Booger water, huh. Do we have any water in the Unit?"

"Yeah, booger water."

I didn't find water back on the board, but I came upon a bottle of white wine, which I opened by inserting the blade of a pocket knife and twisting the cork out. "Rex, do you want some wine?"

"No thanks."

I swallowed down some aspirin and a handful of vitamins. Outside the sun was coming up. Still hallucinating, I found a spot to lie down for a while. We were there for an hour or so before JJ started up the engine. "Everybody on board? Here we go."

The wine had a calming effect and I dozed as we pulled back on the highway and trundled south. I awoke on the downhill side of Raton Pass. JJ was going for it, the Blue Unit swaying dangerously as Mickey crouched sideways in the aisle, pretending he was riding a skateboard. "All right, Boys. Yahoo!"

We stopped for gas at Layton near the Texas line where we picked up a jug of whiskey, some Cokes, a six-pack of beer, tuna, and a loaf of bread. In Santa Fe, in another life, I had gone to school and played football with guys from Raton and Clayton, New Mexico, near the Texas border. Further back, my grandfather—my mom's dad who was born in Ireland—fired boilers on steam trains going over Raton Pass and had raised his family in Las Vegas, New Mexico.

We pulled away as Townes fed tuna to the pitiful Dumpster, Rex and Mary played cards back by the captain's table, and the rest of us were scattered. I drank a couple of beers and slept. Later JJ pulled over to sleep somewhere between Wichita Falls and Fort Worth, where Townes was born. From there on, it was a straight shot down I-35 to Austin.

Uncle Seymour

Seymour Washington, a retired blacksmith, lived in the same house in Clarksville for over forty years while the city of Austin grew up around him. Affectionately known as Uncle Seymour, he was a big man with an easy disposition. His house was a wooden frame affair with dark-papered walls. He had running water in the kitchen, but only an outside privy where his bird dog, Jim, was chained. His other dog, a little terrier that stayed by him, was named Pepe. Unk's front porch featured an assortment of old chairs and a sagging couch. An ancient pick-up truck that had not moved in years rusted in the yard, along with a barbecue smoker made from a fifty-five gallon oil drum. The porch was the focal point, a neighborhood gathering place, where people would stop to pass a few minutes or an afternoon.

I took all this in as I walked down to the corner for a coffee. The neighborhood was alive with a chorus of birdsong, a mockingbird going on like he was king joined by red birds, screaming jays, and shiny black grackles serving up shrieks, chortles, and wheezes. Attracted by a cover story about the fall of Saigon, I picked up a *Newsweek* at the store and brought it back with me. There was also a piece about the twenty-eighth anniversary of the harbor explosion that blew up Texas City. On April 16, 1947 the nitrate freighter Grand Camp caught fire in the harbor. After the first explosion everyone went down to the docks to watch when a second explosion blew them away. Texas City was Rex's home town. The explosion shook buildings twenty miles away in

Houston. Ambulances came from as far away as Dallas.

These and other topics were discussed and debated around Seymour's porch. The group included Townes, Rex, and Chito, an old friend from Townes' shock treatment days in the psychiatric ward in Galveston, and his girlfriend, Mary Ann. We were watching David, a cousin of Seymour's, spreading a load of gravel. Thumbing through the magazine, Townes found a piece that grabbed his attention. "Some cat in New York, right, somebody from Madison Avenue, is telling people over here that this Solzhenitsyn is another Tolstoy. Well, I read *The Gulag* and it just ain't true. He don't even come close." Townes' remark floated out into the morning without comment from the rest.

Uncle Seymour said, "You know Townes, if we had a lot of money we could buy the Free Home Baptist Church and I'll be the preacher."

"But you're rich already, Uncle." Mary Ann was a redhead, redder than Cindy. A guitar was going around and Townes began to sing:

> *This Nine Pound Hammer is a little too heavy*
> *For my size, for my size*
> *Roll on Buddy, don't you roll too slow*
> *How can I roll when the wheels won't go?*

Uncle Seymour appeared to be deep in rumination. "She was so jealous, she always thought I was running off with another woman, which I was," Seymour chuckled to himself. Townes began finger-picking "Deep River Blues" while David attacked the pile of gravel with a will. "He makes that thing talk, don't he?"

Townes, regarding the pile of gravel, "You know if I had thirty years and a sling-shot I could bury Nau's Drug Store from here."

Seymour chuckling. "My, my. That boy has spreaded them two loads of gravel."

Townes: "It's a real pleasure to watch him work."

Seymour began telling us the story of Job. He might have made a good preacher if he hadn't been a blacksmith. He got right into it when the spirit moved him.

"Job was the chosen prophet of God. And the devil told God that he was making hedge—protection—around Job. And Job, he had a lot of children. He had a barn and a lot of cattle. And the barn all burned down, and the children all died. And Job, he got down with sores all over him. And his wife was waiting on him. You know how a woman can wait on a man when he's sick. And his wife said, 'Why don't you cuss God and die?'"

Seymour looked around and somewhere a jay screamed. Townes was working on a pint and I motioned for him to let me have a sip.

"And Job was laying there on his side. And he said, 'You're talking foolish, woman. I'm gonna serve my God until my change comes.' And Job got his barn all back. He raised another family and had all his children, all his cattle and everything."

Seymour paused again and came about on another tack, "Then Jesus Christ was walking through the land. He walked up to a high precipice. And the Devil came up and said, 'If you're the son of God, prove it to me by jumping off this mountain.' And Jesus said, 'You're talking foolishness. Thou shall not test the faith of my God.'"

Townes said, "Stick your finger in a buzz saw."

Seymour continued, "Here's another story, Richard. Jesus Christ walked up the mountain with his cross on his shoulder. He had promised his father he would die that man should have the right. While those Romans was nailing his hands to the cross he said, 'Forgive them, they know not what they do.'"

Seymour's eyes began to fill with tears. "Forgive them. That makes me cry every time I think of it. Because look, if you're punishing me and being real mean to me, why can't I look up to the Lord and say 'Forgive them, they know not what they do.'"

Some Changes

"Are you sure there's nothing wrong with you?" It was my father on the phone in Houston, his tone of voice that was not so much a question as a demand.

"Don't worry, I'm fine. I've just got a cold."

"Well, you sound kind of funny. You're sure you're all right?"

"Really, I'm fine. I'll see you in a few days."

"Your mother and I have been worried."

"Well, tell her not to worry."

In fact, I wasn't so fine. I had walking pneumonia. Things were moving fast with no sign of letting up. For once my luck had changed, and after a long dry spell I was beginning to feel like a man again. I had Maggie the mountain woman to thank for breaking the ice. Then an event occurred which would set wheels in motion and bring on a new chapter in my life. We played a club called Castle Creek and it happened afterwards, while the boys were drinking and gaming in the Unit that I went home with a strange new woman. I didn't realize it at the time, nor when I awoke the next morning. Fair, with raven hair, gray-green eyes, and a butterfly tattoo, she was looking at me as if trying to remember how we had come to wake up together. She had a firm body with nicely formed breasts, the kind you could just cup your hand over. She had a warm smile. "Good morning."

"Damn." I must have given off a whistle of appreciation. "Good morning. Where are we?"

"We're out by the lake."

"So I didn't die and go to heaven?" It was a corny remark, but she only smiled. I lay back looking at the ceiling. Like a fog lifting, my mind began to clear and I remembered a wild ride out of town, and another shuddering ride that caused an aftershock to run through me. In those days things like this could happen; a beautiful woman might take you home and fuck your brains out. Not every night, but now and then you might get lucky. Back in Nashville, sex had become a kind of torture where my nervousness only made things worse and I always came too soon. My nights with the mountain woman were more for warmth and sex. Maggie changed my luck. Things were turning around again and now I felt complete. I felt like a man again.

I didn't try to force things and said good-bye when she dropped me off later that day in Clarksville. Her name was Holly. I had no earthly idea this woman was destined to become my third wife. I was still hopeful then of getting back together with Mary.

Back in Clarksville, a pungent smell surrounded the Blue Unit. Warmer temperatures had finally melted the frozen load hauled down from the Rocky Mountains and beyond. To compound the problem, JJ Wanker had gone off to Houston, leaving it parked across the street from Uncle Seymour's house. Then Mickey and I got into an argument where he aggravated me to the point that I took a swing at him. Mickey wasn't hurt, but I felt bad about losing my temper. Maggie consoled me. "It's only whiskey talking," she said.

The next morning, I caught a ride out to the edge of town and hitchhiked to Houston. After a couple of days at my parents I caught a ride to Nashville. Mary had rented a new place where she let me stay a night on the sofa. And it was there, the day after my birthday, we learned Skinny Dennis had died out in California. He died with his boots on after playing his last show. The news hit me hard. I'm still not even sure how I ended up back in Texas a few days later, or even what happened over the next few weeks.

We continued to hang out at Uncle Seymour's in Clarksville. Townes and Cindy had moved into a trailer a couple of blocks away. After a gig in Houston, we all went down to Mickey's parents' beach house on the Bolivar Peninsula where Rex and I went wade fishing in the surf. An idea began to take hold. "Hey Rex, why don't we move to the beach?"

"Let's do it."

"Really, to hell with the music business."

We were out past the second bar with the water chest high, fishing on the bottom with dead shrimp. I felt a strong pull on my rod and knew I had a good fish on the other end.

"Hey man, what you got?"

"I don't know. He's pulling pretty hard." In a minute or so I brought the fish in closer, a shark about three feet long. The fish made a dive between me and Rex and I screamed while the rod went flying.

"Damn, what's wrong with you?"

"That's a shark, Rex!"

"Yeah, and that's Mickey's father's fishing pole and you just threw away. Now we gotta get it back." Rex reeled in his own line and began casting and retrieving. After a time he managed to snag the line from the lost pole and reel it back in with the shark still attached. The fish was worn out and hardly moved as Rex extracted the hook.

"Man, that thing is three hundred million years old."

Rex glanced at the shark. "This thing, it's just a baby."

"Let's go back and have a drink."

Rex released the shark which swam slowly away. "Let's go."

The water shallowed up to waist high, then got deeper, then shallowed up again as we splashed up to the shore. "Rex, I'm serious, let's move to the beach."

"I'm ready. Let's move to Galveston."

But it would take a while before it all came together. There was an altercation with Townes the next day going back on the ferry. Cindy had poured out all the whiskey and I took it upon myself to complain to him about it, "Man, your old lady is just ruining everything."

Townes' eyes flashed obsidian, "Well, what if I was to say your old lady's a no-good slut?"

I swung at Townes, just grazing him as he jumped back. Then I broke into tears. For the second time in as many weeks, I lost my temper. This time it was Mary—Rex's Mary—who consoled me as I headed towards the back of the ferry with the vague intention of jumping overboard.

"Where are you going?"

"I don't know."

"You weren't going to jump were you?"

"I don't know, I guess not."

I opened a show for Townes and the boys at a new club called The Sweetheart of Texas in Houston on May 15th. There was an auction to raise money for some forgotten cause. I remember I had donated a piece I had saved from the fiddle Townes smashed up in Denver, and that this particular piece never came up for bid. The next night I played a solo gig at the Contemporary Arts Museum. I opened some shows for Kenneth Threadgill around this time, whom I had seen a few years before singing Jimmie Rodgers' songs. Kenneth had white hair with sideburns and a prominent beer belly. A kind of a father figure to Texas musicians, he used to have a beer joint in Austin where he was one of the first to hire Janis Joplin.

Around this time another Kerrville Festival came around, one of the rainy years. Townes played, with Mickey and Rex backing him up. Later, with a full entourage abroad, JJ was doing doughnuts in the muddy parking lot. He managed to stick the Unit two or three times, thereby getting himself banned from the festival for life. There was more. A naked man came aboard and sat down for a drink. Later a man was looking for his woman who had been with the naked man. There was a dice game that lasted until daylight. There was drinking and a thick haze of smoke. Townes ruled. At the center of this manic, saturnalian scene he was the master of all the games, the man who stayed up the latest.

By June I was back in Nashville. Dennis's death brought Mary and me closer together. She agreed to move to Galveston for the summer for a change and a chance to patch things up. True to his word, Rex had found a place at 1313 Church Street. In late June we moved in, Rex and I, and our two Marys.

Island Days

Mary and I left Nashville after her last night working at a Green Hills restaurant called Nero's Cactus Canyon. We may have driven straight through in her Plymouth Duster. It was a good running car that had made the trip a couple of times before, beginning when she had driven down with Rodney, and again after we were married and we drove to Kerrville with Skinny Dennis. She had been terrified when we left the Interstate and took off across two-lane farm and ranch roads. Mary was proud of her car, and I had learned better than to ask her to borrow it. Letting go of my old Volvo turned out to be a worse mistake than I had figured.

But I loved Mary for all that. I loved her with a helpless intensity. No matter that she bored me sometimes. No matter that she never picked up after herself and let her clothes pile up. No matter that I never knew what she was thinking, or her inner soul. If to love is also to suffer, then I loved her twice as hard. I suffered, and I wasn't through with it by half.

The summer started on a good note when our Marys found work at the Café Toriffe down on the Strand. A lot of restoration work was going on there, refurbishing the nineteenth century buildings. There seemed to be the makings of a renaissance in Galveston. In fact, the whole Gulf Coast was booming with the oil business in full swing and lots of rigs drilling offshore. Rex and I didn't immediately go out and find work. We were too busy fishing.

Rex had a seine that we used to catch bait, finger-mullet and mud-minnows, from the sloughs down at the east end of the Island. He had acquired an old Oldsmobile, a four-door with plenty of room, a perfect beach car. We fished nearly every morning from the piers and rock groins along Seawall Boulevard, always catching plenty for a meal. By noon, the heat drove us back to the house on Church Street. Out place wasn't much to look at but came with a boss air conditioner. We passed the hottest part of the day drinking beer and relaxing until evening, when we'd go out and play music at a joint called Gandalf's. It was nearly August before we found work.

We were over on the Bolivar side. Bolivar, where the pregnant Jane Long, her daughter, and Kian, her servant woman, endured the bitter winter of 1821 when the bay froze over and a bear ambled across, their dog nipping at its heels. Walking along the shrimp docks we came upon Johnny Howard, captain of the Part Time, and his rig man, Bud. Gap-toothed and wild in the eye, Johnny looked up when we stepped aboard and Rex made his pitch.

"We're looking for work."

Johnny Howard squinted up from a piece of machinery he had disassembled on the deck. "You guys know anything about shrimping?"

"Yeah, I used to help out my brother-in-law." Rex had never mentioned a brother-in-law to me but I knew he didn't mind trying to get away with a story.

"Do you boys know how to cull?"

"Well, like I said, I used to go out shrimping with my brother-in-law. We used to go out in the bay."

"I said do you know how to cull."

"Well, I have gone shrimping before."

Johnny's attention was now directed to me. "I've never worked on a shrimp boat, but I've worked offshore plenty on drilling rigs."

Johnny looked unimpressed. His partner who had a burly, simian appearance looked on. "I'll tell you what, I'll hire you both on as one man and you can split your share. Maybe the two of you together can do the work of one."

"All right, we'll take it." Rex and I answered as one.

"You guys be here first thing in the morning."

"We'll be here." Rex and I could hardly contain our excitement. We were headed for blue water, the real thing. No more hanging out on the beach.

"One more thing. If you get seasick, we ain't turning around, you got that? I don't care how sick you get. We'll be gone five or six days."

We picked up a six-pack at a one room beer joint by the ferry landing called Zams Famous For Nothing. We pulled onto the ferry line, and I popped open a couple of beers and handed one to Rex. "All right, amigo!"

"We did it. Hey, we're shrimping now. You know I didn't know what he was talking about. What was that word?"

"You mean cull? It means to separate."

"Cull, huh?"

"Yeah, like culling out the trash fish."

"We be culling then."

We rode back across to the Island on the *E. H. Thorton Jr.* Some of these same ferries have been running for forty years or more. I had their names memorized at one time, and one or two of the old ones are still in service. It's probably the best free ferry ride in the world. The first time I remember taking it was as a kid going duck hunting with my dad. You could always see dolphins and some rusty freighter or tanker headed in or out from Houston.

We did not look so prosperous in the old Olds, and you might not think to look at us that we would have had much reason to feel so pleased with ourselves, but Rex and I rode back to the Island proud to be able to tell our two Marys that we had found ourselves a real job of honest work. And one, incidentally, where we figured the fishing had to be pretty good.

The Part Time

It was mid-afternoon before we headed out the next day, after shopping for groceries and supplies, topping off the fuel, and filling the holds with shaved ice blown in with a high-pressure hose. Leaving the dock, we swung into the channel with the Galveston skyline across from us. Heading for the jetties, we lowered the outrigger booms and then the stabilizers as the *Part Time* nosed into the swells and I thrilled at the taste of salt spray. Johnny was at the wheel while Rex and I stayed out on the deck helping Bud, a burly, taciturn man with slicked down black hair.

But an unlucky star hung over the *Part Time* and over Johnny Howard, lately of Apalachicola, Florida. Johnny, who lived in a trailer with no septic tank in a soggy marsh by the Intracoastal Canal behind Crystal Beach, whose luck on this trip ran out—as did all our luck—an hour into the first drag of the evening when the engine froze up. There was nothing to do but sleep until daylight and wait for the Coast Guard to tow us in. We had one serious problem: how to get the nets back on board without power.

We awoke to the creaking of gear as the *Part Time* rocked in the swell with the nets hanging straight down from the booms on either side. Using a pipe wrench with a cheater pipe for increased leverage, we began to winch up the nets an inch at a time. Well acquainted with this kind of work from my oilfield experience, I cursed our luck. I guessed the task at hand would take us many hours. A hot sun was coming up over slick, glassy swells.

"You know, this is going to take us forever."

Johnny looked disgusted. "You got any bright ideas?"

Rex, "Yeah, let's get a hacksaw and cut the nets loose."

"Them nets and doors is worth over five thousand dollars and we ain't cutting 'em loose."

In fact, I did have an idea after the Coast Guard cutter hove to, after first boarding us and taking a perfunctory look around for drugs or weapons. They eased off a ways, waiting to tow us back to shore. "Hey Johnny, let's get them to pull up our nets. If they've got a block on board we can run the cables through. They can pull forward and then back towards us while we pull up the slack."

"Yeah, it might work."

Somewhat to my surprise, it did, though we still had some hard going. Neither the Coast Guard nor the *Part Time* had a block on board and we were forced to improvise with a big shackle. The cutter managed to raise the nets a little at a time, backing towards us as we pulled the snarled coils onto the deck. After a time, we got one net and set of boards laid down on top of the mess, and the outrigger boom raised and tied into place with Johnny grumbling and swearing. "Stupid bastards. We don't haul them booms up 'till we're inside the jetties."

Grunting with effort and the sweat pouring off of us, we brought in the other net and nearly had the outrigger tied in place when it gave way and fell with a tremendous crash exactly where Rex had been standing. He could move fast for a klutz. You wouldn't believe Rex could walk through a door without banging into it, yet he made a ten foot leap into the wheel house just as the boom fell crashing across it in a shower of rust. Truly, there was a saving grace about Rex that belied his clumsiness. After a time he poked his head out and glanced around.

"You okay Rex?"

"Yeah, I thought I was a goner." Rex brushed himself off, squinting in the sunlight.

"Man, I did too."

Captain Johnny Howard laughed raucously from back in the

stern while Bud gave off a slow grin. "Ha ha. I never seen anybody move so fast."

When the dust cleared, we tied off the port side outrigger where it lay across the wheelhouse roof. Someone from the cutter threw us a line with the heavier line attached, and we tied it on at the bow. The Coast Guard towed us back to Port Bolivar in ignominy and embarrassment. Back on the Island, our Marys were surprised to see us returning so soon. Our first trip had been a bust but we had proven our mettle in a crisis. Sure enough, in a few days with the engine repaired and the boom refitted back in place, we were headed out the jetties again to resume our shrimping careers.

Jaws

"Hey, Rex. Let's cut this thing loose and get some rest."

Rex had a big one on he had been fighting for what seemed like twenty minutes. Each time he pumped it up near the boat, it sounded again. "No way man. I ain't letting this baby go."

Rex was fishing with a boat rod and a Penn star-drag reel that had been in my family since way back in the fifties. Practically an antique, it was still in good shape. There is, or was, a picture of me holding it and a jackfish I could scarcely lift, taken down the coast at Port Aransas when I was nine or ten. Not only a good offshore fishing rig, it was a link to my past. We'd started catching fish with it right away, our morning recreation after dragging for shrimp all night. Even Johnny Howard got into it. He had been fishing from boats all his life but to our amazement had never used sporting tackle.

On this morning we were into a bunch of sharks and had figured to make ourselves some extra money. The weather was fresh and overcast with swells running six to eight feet, the anchor line taut and humming. We had finished culling the last drag of the night, put the shrimp on ice, and rinsed off the decks, taking care to save back a few of the sand trout for bait. Johnny and Bud had already gone off to their bunks to sleep. Rex and I had four or five sharks on the deck, big ones five or six feet long. Our plan was to cut out the jaws, cook away the meat and sell them to the tourists.

"Hey Rex, don't you think we got enough?"

"Hold it, I've got a big one on here."

"Well, bring him in."

"I can't." Rex was tiring. Each time he pumped the fish up near the boat it sounded again.

"Why don't we just cut him loose?"

"No way, José. This baby's mine."

After a time, Rex brought the fish up close by the stern and made the line fast. Then I held him by the legs hanging upside-down while he gaffed the fish using a longshoreman's cargo hook to snag it. Our other gaff, which had been tied to a boat hook, was already lost, torn from Johnny's hand earlier that morning. Somehow, Rex managed to hang on and we brought the shark aboard, snapping and thrashing on the deck.

"All right!" Rex was flushed and triumphant. We clubbed the shark, rendering it shuddering and harmless. I was ready to turn in, but Rex was too excited to quit. "Come on, man, just one more."

"Okay, you go ahead."

The wind was picking up and whitecaps were surging as he baited up with a sand trout, letting it spool off into the current. He snapped the drag just as the rod bent over and a hundred yards of line sang off the reel. A great silver shape rose out of the waves, shaking and tearing itself loose, a sailfish or a marling, we were never sure.

Rex reeled in the empty line. "Wow, did you see that?" He whistled, shook his head. "That's the biggest fish I ever saw."

We made brief, bloody work cutting out the jaws, throwing the carcasses back over the side. There wasn't any market for shark meat then. We rinsed off the back deck, stashed the jaws below in the ice hold, and turned in. There were only three bunks on the *Part Time*. I dragged out a grimy mattresses and placed it crossways in the wheelhouse, where I fell asleep immediately.

Late that afternoon we boiled the shark jaws, just like in the movie. Except in real life, the teeth all fell to the bottom of the pot while the cartilage that had held them in place dissolved into soup. Sharks, I remembered, had no bones. There are not nearly so many sharks around these days, but you can still buy jaws in the souvenir shops. It's a mystery to me how they preserve them intact to sell to the tourists.

Endangered Species

One early morning in September we were dragging off the Bolivar coast, just a few hundred yards from the breakers on our port side. The water was sandy and streaked with foam. A cool morning, with rain squalls under scudding clouds. It would have been rough but for the nets and stabilizers that smoothed out the ride as the *Part Time* pulled steadily against the surge of the waves. We had been offshore all night, trawling for brown shrimp, and had run in at dawn to try our luck with the jumbo, or white shrimp, close to the beach.

I could feel the adrenaline pumping as we dumped the first load on the deck and put the nets back overboard. There is always a moment of anticipation when the bags spill open and you behold the wonder of what you've brought up from the bottom. Seafood lovers who presume to take the high moral ground over meat eaters would do well to consider the mass death caused by trawling the sea floor for crustaceans. Seated on short stools, we set to work culling with hoe-shaped scrapers, separating the shrimp from a slithering pile of dead and dying fish: croakers, sand trout, small flounder, ribbonfish, sharks, rays, hard head catfish, and scuttling crabs. We worked fast while the auto-pilot kept us on a steady course parallel to the shore.

Down below us cruised the jackfish, like a menacing phalanx of outlaw bikers. Early in the trip, we'd pinch the heads off the shrimp because they lasted longer on ice, but now we dropped the shrimp into plastic baskets, heads on. From time to time, we'd take a larger, long-handled scraper and push a pile of discarded fish out through the scuppers. They were met instantly in a churning, slashing attack as the jackfish tore into them, while a school of black tip sharks behind them would rip the water to a froth as they devoured what was passing back to them.

As we worked on the diminishing pile, I began to sense that there was something moving underneath it, though at first I could see nothing more than fish and crabs. Gradually, a turtle took shape. On its back, it began working its flippers as soon as they were free, flailing frantically, trying to swim in a sea of air. We could see the creature's eyes beginning to bloody as it slapped itself repeatedly. I looked at Rex. Johnny and Bud had gone forward.

"You know this turtle is probably an endangered species. Maybe we ought to throw it back overboard."

"Yeah man, I agree. Let's go talk to Johnny."

We pushed the rest of the trash fish overboard and rinsed the deck with the saltwater hose. We rinsed the baskets of shrimp and handed them down to Bud in the ice hold, where he spread them out on a bed of shaved ice with another layer to cover them. We replaced the hatch cover and placed a canvas tarp over it. The turtle remained on deck. Often drowned in shrimp nets, this one was still plenty alive. Johnny came back out on deck. Rex and I exchanged glances but I let him do the talking. "Hey Johnny, maybe we ought to throw this turtle back overboard. This thing is probably endangered."

Captain Johnny Howard looked at Rex. One of the most primitive men I ever met, Johnny claimed to have done time in a Florida penitentiary for carving up a man's face with an oyster shell. He had thinning hair and eyes of a wild, indeterminate color. He was sharpening a homemade knife that looked as if it had been fashioned out of a leaf from an automobile spring. He looked around with his gap-toothed grin, "Ha ha! You better believe this here fucker is endangered." In one fell motion, Johnny reached down and cut off its head.

Memory fails me at this point. Not normally queasy, I may have gone and laid down on one of the filthy bunks and closed my eyes for a few minutes while Johnny, Bud, and Rex were out on the back deck. I guessed they were cutting up the turtle. We were still close enough to the shore to make out the traffic on the coast road, or maybe I only imagined it, there just beyond the ragged tops of the waves. The road is now closed to traffic past the turnoff to High Island and Winnie. The Gulf is claiming it back, though I hear you can still get through with four-wheel drive.

Johnny came forward with his hands full of turtle meat, which he had cut into chunks. He turned on the burner and soon had hot oil bubbling in a large cast iron skillet. A strange, enticing aroma began to drift through the galley. "Smells great," I said. "Yeah, help yourself, but we're gonna pick up the nets here pretty quick." I rolled out of the bunk and went forward to where Johnny had placed the cooked turtle on a plate. We had been feasting all summer on seafood, first on pan fish, trout, and flounder we caught on the beach. At the Café Torrife, our Marys would slip us free beers and grill kingfish fillets we brought in from the boat. But this was utterly different. It was meat, light, with a delicate texture and a faint taste of the sea. I must have wolfed down half a dozen pieces by myself. In fact, I've never, before or since, tasted anything as sublime as the flesh of that hapless creature

Gandalf's

About the time Rex and I were shrimping, there was a hippie beer joint down on Seawall Boulevard, not far from where it intersects with Broadway. Located on the second floor, it was called Gandalf's, run by a fellow whose name I don't remember, but who looked a lot like Gandalf. The bar, tables, and benches all had a homemade, patched-together look, as if they had been assembled from scraps and driftwood. There was a tiny stage where we used to play. It had a PA of sorts, with the speakers stacked on tea boxes from the Lipton factory and the microphones taped to broom handles.

After a few trips, Johnny Howard figured Rex and I had learned enough to start alternating trips as deckhands. So it happened that I was out on the boat on the afternoon that Rex was playing at Gandalf's when Willie Nelson and Darrell Royal wandered in. Darrell Royal, the famous University of Texas football coach, was known for saying, "There are three things that can happen when you throw a football, and two of them are bad." As for Willie, he hadn't yet become a household name, but he was at least nearly famous. It's hard to say what they were doing at Gandalf's. They had come down for a golf tournament and were just hanging out.

Rex finished his set and leaned his guitar against the wall. He was headed for the bar when Willie complimented him, "That was some real nice singing."

"Why thank you sir. I appreciate that." While Rex walked over for his beer, Darrell and Willie finished theirs and exited down the stairs.

There were only a few people in the room but they had all recognized the distinguished visitors. "Hey Rex," said Gandalf, "Don't you know who that was?"

"No, who was it?"

"That was Willie Nelson."

"You're kidding."

"That was Willie Nelson and Darrell Royal."

"Man, I can't believe it. I can't believe I didn't recognize him. He even complimented me on my singing."

It was strange that Rex didn't recognize Willie, as he was a fan and even sang a couple of Nelson songs. But this was before Willie perfected his outlaw look, or maybe he had come down to the Island disguised as a golfer. As for Gandalf's, it shut down after a few months. There may have been trouble with the beer permit, or maybe Gandalf himself moved on. There's a Mario's Pizza restaurant there today.

Later, there was another club we used to play down on Seventh and Winnie, The Gangplank. It was run by two guys named Bob and Charlie from somewhere up north. Not a place for the timid, it drew a raucous crowd of shrimpers, bikers, hippie carpenters, and short-haired guys from the Coast Guard. While it didn't have any chicken wire around the stage, there were nights we could have used some. The cops eventually shut the Gangplank down, or at least saw to it that no more live music could be played there.

About this time, Rex and I began to devise plans for our bait camp, beer joint, and honky-tonk retirement center. With a funky PA and some speakers stacked on tea boxes maybe, where we might fish and drink and play music at night. Rex kept the dream alive, saving money from his job selling cardboard boxes up in Houston. Now he says he's waiting on me to admit I'm not going to make it in the music business. Which is perspicacious of him, to use a word you won't often hear in country music.

Rex's own songs are way too left-of-center for Nashville. I told him so once, suggesting he might try his hand at writing commercially. "It might be good for you to try," I said.

"You mean I would have to write more songs I don't like?"

"Your songs are too weird," I said, remembering some song writing advice I had heard once up in Tennessee. "You've got to write so the night manager at the Exxon station understands you."

"You mean an Iranian?" Rex never did care much for Nashville. His favorite songwriter these days is Tom Waits, which is all he listened to in his car. Rex even named his dog Tom.

September Logs

2 SEPTEMBER 1975: Loaded up with fuel, oil, gas, ice and groceries. Cleared the jetties about 2:00 PM. Headed ssw in a light rolling swell. Fixed dinner of pork steak with ketchup, onion-garlic sauce, canned green beans, and boiled potatoes. We're somewhere off Freeport in 15 or 16 fathoms. Johnny says we can hope to catch a few big shrimp and maybe not too much trash. How he figures this, I don't know. The fathometer is out of order and we don't have a chart for this area. Winging it, as usual.

3 SEPT: Drags last night netted one box or so of big tails. About a three hundred dollar night. Anchored ssw of Freeport. Radio playing, Johnny and Budd sleeping. Lying on my filthy mattress, stays creaking and groaning as the boards swing back and forth. Fixed scrambled eggs for breakfast. Polish sausage with home fries. Case of the runs.

Later, after sleeping, some flycatchers came aboard this afternoon, driven on a north wind. Also, many biting flies. Birds catching flies but not all of them. Hot, sultry night with lightning flashes across the horizon. Occasional rumbles of thunder. Shrimp running smaller tonight. Starting to squall. Earlier, tried to give the birds some fresh water. No telling if they're still around. Cooked chicken tonight, a little underdone, but Johnny and Bud said nothing.

4 SEPT: Caught about two boxes last night, pulling in the last drag without rinsing the nets, the water being full of sharks. They can't tear up the nets when you're pulling up a ball of mud, though it makes for harder culling. Johnny caught a kingfish while Bud and I were icing down the shrimp. I suspect this chemical powder we put on them is probably bad for you. All the shrimpers use it.

Smoked some homegrown after a breakfast of hash, eggs, and bacon. Laying in the wheelhouse with an electric fan blowing down on me. Small fleet of boats around us fishing for kingfish. Falling asleep, I get a hard-on dreaming I'm making love to a friend of my wife's. Falling asleep again, leaving my own stain on the tick. Late afternoon, Johnny breaks out a package of cookies and eats all but four. He says you can't fill a grave on a crescent moon. There won't be enough dirt to fill it. Try on a full moon and you will have too much dirt. Fixed spaghetti for dinner. Hard boiling some eggs for later.

5 SEPT 1:00 AM: Try-net broke on the second check earlier. Brought in one haul with lots of fish, not too good, maybe three quarters of a basket. Standing wheel watch, running NE-SW, an hour each way. A clear night with lots of stars, the lights of Freeport glowing on the horizon. Once a man becomes aware of his fate, why can't he accept it? Why should knowledge make him afraid? Time and space, infinity and death. And roaches, crawling all over the boat, big one just ran down my leg. Cockroaches in the cupboards, so many places to hide. Death to roaches!

Later: Put up two boxes last night. Began raining about dawn. Pancakes for breakfast. Fished a while with Bud and Johnny. Still raining when I fell asleep.

6:30 PM: Cooked fried chicken. Johnny and Bud are mending nets. Went aft and caught a bonita and a kingfish. Wind out of ESE and freshening. Sun in decline with a rainbow. Shrimp fleet all around. Moments of beauty, solitude, boredom. Thinking about Skinny Dennis, gone nearly half a year.

6 sept 2:00 am: Dragging off San Luis Pass, ne-sw. Made a little over a box the first drag. Just beat the rain getting the deck cleared and washed and the shrimp in the hold.

3:00 am: Turned around to sw, rain letting up a bit. Glow on the horizon on starboard side, lights of the fleet off to the port. We're working inshore, alone. Once you become aware of your death, your life will never be the same. No stars tonight as we chug through the darkness in a light swell.

3:45 pm: Disappointing catch last night, box and a half at most. Lots of trash and croakers. Running without try-trawl or fathometer a shot in the dark. Lots of shark damage the last two hauls. Bored, tired of having to drag my grungy mattress into the wheelhouse to sleep every morning. Had a dream Townes and I were driving around Montreal. He killed a snake, and after some effort, succeeded in throwing it out of the car. Townes freaked out and took off his shirt, checking for bites. There were none. He said to me. "You do a guest set tonight."

Later: Worse than faggots, these redneck-repressed queers themselves, all the time talking about sucking dicks. Pussy spoken of only in the pejorative sense—fear of women. This or violence. Boring, boring. We all form the circle. Life coming to be, life passing. The form is a vessel which may also shatter. Broken shards of lost tribes, civilizations, religions, species, eco-systems, planets, suns, galaxies. Sunset, running to the east. Rice and beans on the stove, flounder dusted in cornmeal.

7 sept 5:00 am: Sunday. Dragging wnw, following another boat. Looks like a two-box night. Easy culling with little trash. Somewhere off Galveston. If we total nine boxes tonight we'll have half our intended goal.

10:30 am: Caught two big sharks over six feet. Rough seas. Made our two boxes.

8:00 PM: Woke up this afternoon to find our anchor line snapped while we slept. Took our time running inshore. Going to drag back to Galveston, maybe get a night on the bank.

8 SEPT 2:00 AM: Fishing in eight fathoms, running ENE-SSW. Fairly good catch so far, including close to half a basket of jumbo white shrimp. We're somewhere between San Luis Pass and Galveston. Johnny says if the white shrimp are running we're going to fish around the clock and won't need an anchor. Lots of croaker and hardheads. We have to bring the nets up every two hours instead of three.

Taking the wheel watch, along comes the thought, should I go overboard. Johnny and Bud might sleep for hours. A good way to get recycled but I hang on to this leaky old tub, literally, for life. Moving off to the east, still marking eight fathoms.

9 SEPT 8:00 AM: Running towards Galveston. Green water, overcast sky. Rain and a double rainbow after a psychedelic sunrise.

10:00 AM: Came across two boats working. Dropped our nets and try-trawl, the latter coming aboard half hour later with fifty big whites, the most I've ever seen. We may be in the money.

5:00 PM: Tied up behind the Ruth Sullivan, another trawler out of Port Bolivar. Jack up rig nearby. Made a little over a box of whites this morning. Second drag yielded nothing but fish. We're down to one bin of ice left in the hold. Enough to fish tonight, tomorrow at the most. Altogether, we've got eleven or twelve boxes of tails now, One and a half boxes of whites.

11:00 PM: Taking the first watch, following another boat, headed SE in seven fathoms. Johnny and Bud asleep. Seas choppy, night clear.

10 SEPT 2:00 AM: Johnny decided to split back to the jetties, a four hour run against a strong current. My share for this trip: about three hundred dollars.

Chef Rex

Cooking was the deckhand's job on the *Part Time*. Johnny made the decisions and ran the boat while Bud ran the winches, and together they took care of the nets and the gear. Not what you would call finicky eaters, they were no problem to cook for. Johnny could come up with pretty tasty one pot meals, but considered it his due to be served. Enter Rex, who had advanced to grilling meat and was starting on fish. "I need a lesson. Johnny wants me to start cooking."

"You know how to scramble eggs, right?"

"Sure, I can do eggs. I need a few tips."

"Okay. First you'll want to serve them hash browns for breakfast."

"I just fry them, right?"

"Make some boiled potatoes the night before. Make plenty so you'll have extra left over for the morning. Cut them up in pieces and cut up an onion. Fry them together in bacon grease and serve them with eggs."

"Okay, I'll try it."

"That will get you started."

I didn't think any more about Rex, or if I did, I didn't remember our conversation after he went back out. I worked on some songs on my days off: a Leonard Cohen inspired waltz called "Mirrors of Darkness," and a goofy throwaway called "Swamp Rat." Mary and I drove up to Houston to visit my parents for a couple of days. Mary liked my folks. You wouldn't think there was anything wrong between us to see how she acted around them. A few days later, Rex came in and we brought a jug to celebrate his return.

"How was your trip?" I asked.

"Pretty good. We did okay but Johnny's back to cooking again. He fired me as cook."

"What happened?"

"Well, the first night I saved back some boiled potatoes just like you said. Then in the morning I chopped up an onion along with the potatoes. I heated up some grease in the skillet, right—at least I thought it was grease—and made hash browns. I served it to them and Johnny started screaming 'What the fuck is this?' He and Bud were about to puke."

"What'd you do, poison them?"

"Well, I thought it was a can of bacon grease. It turned out to be a can of Go-Jo hand cleaner that I fried the hash browns in. Johnny didn't let me cook anymore after that."

September Logs II

SEPT 20: Many small victories might pass through a man's life unnoticed that, taken together, could make his life worthwhile. We had a close call last night dragging off Bolivar not far from the beach. Almost ran aground and lost the boat. Out on the deck culling, we didn't notice that the auto-pilot had gone out. With a south wind pushing us into the surf, the port stabilizer actually hit bottom.

21 SEPT 2:00 AM: Full moon, clear night and gentle seas. Running in tomorrow because we're nearly out of fuel for the bilge pump. Feel the moon stirring me tonight, to what end or purpose, I don't know.

2:45 PM: Starting to squall after hot, brassy skies all morning. Wheelhouse full of stinging flies. Pump motor filled with the last of our gasoline. We're anchored near the ship channel, so I guess it doesn't matter so much. Rolled a smoke, some homegrown mixed with Oaxacan. Stoned, tired. Can't sleep for the fucking flies, and I've got the first watch tonight.

22 SEPT 3:00 AM: Busted a tickler chain on the first drag. We're going in.

24 SEPT: Back offshore. Tickler chain fixed. So called because it drags through the mud just ahead of the net, 'tickling' the shrimp to jump up and get swept into the net. We've got gasoline for the bilge pump. Now, running down towards Freeport, the generator went out just before dark. Norther blowing in. Fathometer also broken.

25 SEPT: Mottled, bruise-colored skies with foam-streaked seas running eight to twelve feet. Only made one drag before it got too rough to fish. Couldn't make Galveston so we turned downwind and ran into Freeport. Tied up in the Brazos River close to the highway bridge. Bud and Johnny gone to town to get some gear at the surplus store, so they said. They spent some time getting all gussied up, and I think they're up to something. Later, a cool afternoon. Lots of boats in port with more headed up the river all the time. First, a Norther, and now Hurricane Eloise headed for the coast somewhere. Tides five feet above normal. Waves up to twelve feet offshore. Freshening wind blowing whitecaps across the river. Railroad tankers lined up at the Dow Chemical plant. Smoking a joint, listening to Bud's radio.

26 SEPT 3:00 PM: Pulled out of Freeport, alternator repaired. Blue sky day with choppy seas. Air fresh, a little cool. We're dragging within sight of the beach near a jack-up rig. Made a tour of beer joints last night and took in a movie. Police cruisers everywhere picking up shrimpers, drunk or only partly so. According to the lady taxi driver who took us back to the dock, the cops make a lot of money off of the boat crews.

11:30 PM: My watch 'til 3:00 AM. Dragging SW-NE, we're picking up a few shrimp, mostly small ones. Put on coffee water to heat and started the bilge pump. The *Part Time* leaking worse than ever. It takes only ninety minutes before the water reaches the shaft, which stars slinging it all over the engine room. As for the engine itself, we have a leak in the oil cooling system which is getting oil into the water. Water is also leaking from the head gasket in two places and getting into the oil. Also one of our mast stays is loose. Waning moon out, you can catch it in your left hand. Clear night with a light, cool breeze.

Re-reading Gabriel Marquez' *One Hundred Years of Solitude*. Meditating on life and death of the sea creatures we drag up. Funny how a sense of awe and wonder gives way to a fear of the vast unknown. If what comes into being is good, the dissolution of the form is also good. One cannot with clear conscience embrace life and reject death. Says the mind. Ah, but the heart never wants to die.

27 SEPT 11:00 AM: We hit a wreck last night. Worked three or four hours trying to get loose. Nearly put the outrigger under the water to no effect. Chained the cable to the stern, then pulled until I thought we were going to tear the transom clean off. We finally pulled free, brought up our net, somebody else's lost net, and a long piece of pipe from the wrecked boat's cooling system. Far from being pissed off, Johnny and Bud are elated. Apparently, the keel cooler is worth good money as salvage. I know the net is worth some money too, but I don't expect to see any. I don't figure into their venal calculations. We dumped the whole mess on deck and went to bed.

28 SEPT: Up at dawn to cull and clean up the mess, pulled the spare net out of the hold to replace the badly torn one from last night. Dragging off the beach.

11:20 PM: Engine's about to go out on us. We're anchored just off Galveston; going in tomorrow. Sat up an hour or so tonight telling stories and drinking beer. Doors creaking and swinging from the blocks, water lapping against the hull, cheap alarm clock ticking away the hours. Thoughts drifting back to the music world ashore.

Making Tracks

One thing marred the perfection of beach life, and that was my broken heart. Daily, I could see Mary growing more homesick for the hills of Middle Tennessee. She hated fishing and wouldn't go swimming because the salt water was too sticky. She not only hated the feeling of sand on her skin, but she had a phobia that it might somehow work its way inside her. She hated flat, open Texas country, and the Hill Country too because it wasn't green enough. In spite of this I still loved her and she knew it. I also found out she was seeing some medical student when I was out on the boat. Maybe it was only a flirtation. I didn't know. We had come to the Island for one last try to patch things up between us, but I was beginning to see there was no hope in it.

"I want to go home."

"But this is home. Home is where we are."

"Well, it's not for me. I'm tired of this place. I want to go back to Nashville."

"You want to go back. You think Nashville is the center of the universe. You're so provincial I can't believe it."

"I can't help it. I want to go home."

We began fighting terribly. I began to think that she hated me because her father had died young, leaving her to be raised by her mother, who had never remarried. She didn't know how to treat a man, I figured. One night, overcome with shame and impotent rage, I broke a favorite fishing rod, snapping it into pencil length pieces.

Rex took me to task the next day. "I can't believe you broke that pole."

"I had my reasons."

"You should have given it to me. That was a perfectly good fishing pole. I could have used it."

"Yeah, I know it was. It meant a lot to me too, that's why I broke it."

The pole had belonged to my first wife. We bought it on the road up in Oregon after we had come back from the Peace Corps, when we had the Volvo. I took it with me after we split up in Michigan, at the end of the sixties. It was a long time before I tried marriage again. Now the Volvo was gone and the fishing pole was gone and another marriage was headed straight for the rocks. I felt rotten and miserable.

The only place to shake my despair was offshore, where I took my unanswerable questions. Once we cleared the jetties my troubles fell away behind me. What does life mean, anyway? We hold onto notions, and they fly away like tiny birds. I had been hooked on boats since childhood when all I needed was a piece of one-by-four sawed into a point. On top of this, I nailed blocks of wood. A notch cut in the stern could be fitted with a rubber band to which I fixed a tiny paddle. When I was eight, my family moved to Holland, crossing the Atlantic on the *Westerdam*, a ship of the Holland America Line. The crossing lasted seven glorious days. Already, I had longed for a life at sea. Things might have been simple but I had a jealous mistress, and that, of course, was music.

Rex and I quit Johnny Howard and the *Part Time* sometime in October. I think it was around this time that Rex got a job playing bass in a country band at his brother's club in Kemah, up on the bay. Or he and Mary may have moved to Austin around this time. In any event, we decided to let our place go in Galveston. I was working on new plans that had started taking shape when I ran into Rock Romano, an old college friend.

A long-time figure in the Houston music scene, Rock had been playing since high school, fronting rock, R&B, and jazz bands.

Rock had engineered my very first demo tapes a few years before. I told him about an idea that was beginning to take hold, the notion of making my own record. "Hey Rock, how would you like to be my producer?"

"Sure. Are you thinking of making a single?"

"Why don't we go ahead and make a whole album? I've got the songs."

"Sounds good to me. I know a guy who's got an eight-track studio where we might get a deal on time. I'll check with him and see what he says."

And so began my recording career. The more I thought about it, the more excited I became. Another college friend named Mayo Thompson had started an art-rock band called the Red Crayola, which had put out a couple of albums back in the sixties. I hung out at Jack Clement's studio in Nashville when Townes was making his *Late Great* album, and had watched some of the recording of Guy Clark's *Texas Cooking*. The fact that I had neither record contract nor budget was no deterrent. The money would come from somewhere. Rock and I began discussing musicians and songs. We decided to use his band along with Mickey White on acoustic guitar.

This proved to be a good choice, since Mickey was familiar with my material and made an effective band leader while Rock played bass from the control room.

Our first session took place in November at Ramparts Studio in Houston. It was cold and we kept having to turn off the noisy electric heater every time we went for a take. I was awed by the magnitude of the job we had undertaken. In spite of having spent time around studios in Nashville, I didn't know much about making a record. Still, I was in good hands, and by December we had the basic tracks to seven songs in the can. I flew back to Nashville in December. Mary had rented a nice apartment where she let me stay but wouldn't make love.

"You know we're still married."

"I know, but I just can't."

"I wish I didn't love you so much."

"I love you, but it just won't work."

"I know you're fucking somebody else."

She shook her head, looking sad and hopeless. I moved in with Rodney for a few days. He had a spare bedroom in a house that was due to be razed to make room for an expansion of Vanderbilt University. Rodney's career was going great guns. He had just come back from Canada, where he told me he had been invited to join a new band with Emmylou Harris. It was about this time the movie *Heartworn Highways* was being filmed, produced by Jim Szalapski, who was a friend of Skinny Dennis. There is one part of the film with Guy and Susanna Clark, Rodney, Steve Earle, and Steve Young all sitting around trading songs at Guy and Susanna's house in Mount Juliet. I had a small part singing "Hard by the Highway" that ended up on the cutting room floor. Other parts of the movie shot around Nashville included a Larry Jon Wilson studio session, David Allan Coe singing at the state prison, and a Charlie Daniels concert.

There is a poignant scene at the end of the session where Rodney leads the group singing "Silent Night." I have no memory of Christmas itself, not the first one I'd ever spent alone. A few days later, I caught a ride back to Texas with songwriter Bill Calorie. Bill had just got a song cut by Willie Nelson, and we were headed for the big Willie and Waylon Jennings blowout at the Summit in Houston. It seemed like I had put a lot of miles behind me in the year since that frozen night behind the Mangy Moose, at the captain's table in the Blue Unit.

Late in January I drove up to Austin, where Rock and I recorded two more songs in a late night session at Onion Audio, a studio in the basement of the old Armadillo World Headquarters. The next night, I slept over at Townes and Cindy's trailer in Clarksville. A blue norther had come in the night before, and the morning came up brilliant and clear with frost on the windows. We were up early, talking about driving to the feed store for some dog food and laying mash for Townes' chickens. We drank black coffee while Cindy rolled a joint of big-taste Oaxacan pot. We waited until nine, when the feed store opened.

Townes and I drove over to the store and loaded up. We were headed back when he asked, "What time is it?"

"Nine twenty-seven."

"Thanks," Townes fell silent, driving carefully, with almost exaggerated caution. Then he said, "We got thirty more big ones."

"How's that?" For a second I didn't understand, and then I got it. We had thirty more minutes to wait until the liquor store opened.

Back at the trailer, Cindy was watching a game show on television. Languid and stoned, long-legged and freckled with red hair, she seemed more relaxed and at ease than the year before. I always felt a little sorry for Townes' women, with all they had to put up with. They day was warming up with the sun coming through the open door, blinding white on the cinder blocks supporting the television. I was focusing on the textured surfaces of the trailer interior, the imitation walnut sliding and the plastic counters. Townes began sweeping the room with a flourish, the premier song-poet of our generation, waltzing with a broom.

When our thirty minutes were up we hoofed it down to the liquor store, taking the long way around Uncle Seymour's place so Chito or some other thirsty neighbor would be less likely to spot us. Geraldine, the mixed shepherd-husky came along, stopping to say hello and sniff asses with all the dogs. We didn't see any people on the street. At the liquor store, we bought a pint of Old Grand-Dad and walked back the long way to the trailer. Townes showed me around the weedy back yard where he had taken the film crew that had come to Austin after Nashville. "Let me show you where the giant rabbits dragged me down the hole," he said. He lifted up some boards, revealing a subterranean tunnel. "That's where he dragged me in." He told me the crew had spent an entire morning filming around Clarksville, and that they had done some shooting over at Uncle Seymour's.

Townes must have gotten a royalty check in the mail because that afternoon he decided to buy a new guitar. He had lost a fine

D-35 Martin a few months before in a bar on Westheimer in Houston and had since been using borrowed instruments. We drove down to a music store where he picked out a big blond Epiphone with a maple back and sides, a spruce top, and a rosewood fingerboard. A little tinny and new sounding, but it had lots of flash. Back at the trailer, we nipped at the Old Grand-Dad while Townes changed strings. Outside, the light mellowed. The day had warmed considerably, and the air was still. A few chickens scratched about the yard. Cindy rolled another joint.

Townes seemed restless and suggested we go see the film *The Man Who Would Be King*, a Rudyard Kipling tale with lots of scenery and romantic adventure. On the way back, we bought a jug, a fifth this time, which we started working on as soon as we got back to the trailer. We played a few songs. Later, over Cindy's protest, Townes brought in his rooster named Garf. He put a plate down on the floor with a selection of bread crumbs, dog food, and laying mash.

"Dammit, Townes, he's going to shit all over the floor."

"Shh, don't talk that way. He can hear you."

I stayed two days with Townes and Cindy. A couple of days later, he played a gig at a club called Dean Scots in Houston. The next two days I was down with a cold and rested at my parents' house. My notes mention a show at the Old Quarter, though I don't remember it. The following week, Rock and I went back up to Austin, where we put down more tracks at Onion Audio. One of the songs we did was called "Bus Stop Coffee," a tune written by Skinny Dennis. I decided to call the record *In Texas Last December*, after one of the songs on the album.

As for the blond guitar, Townes later shot it full of holes with his .357 magnum. This was after he and Cindy had moved to Nashville, to a farm west of town in Williamson Country. Later still, he used the same gun to play Russian roulette, spinning the cylinder and pulling the trigger. I wasn't there. Townes did it, he told me, to run off Steve Earle. He said Steve, a non-stop talker under any circumstance, was wired on speed and pestering him unmercifully. You might say Steve nearly pestered him to death. Townes said he spun the cylinder again. He said at the second click Steve turned white as a ghost and fled.

This incident undoubtedly scared Townes as well, because shortly afterward he gave the .357 to Steve Young, who lost it to a junkie who broke into his house. As for Steve Earle, his career would later eclipse Townes', and everybody else's, before he began his own descent into madness. I don't know what eventually became of the blond guitar. But one funny thing was that the bullet holes didn't even affect the sound.

Nashville

Rock and I finished overdubbing tracks for the album around the first of March. We decided to take the rough mixes to Nashville to test the waters and see if anyone might be interested. On arrival we camped at Bidey Lomax's house in an upscale West Nashville neighborhood. Bidey was a stout woman who loved to cook and party. Estranged from her husband, John Lomax, nephew of the folk song collector Alan Lomax, she lived with their young son, John Nova. Bidey loved music and always kept the house open for homeless artists and songwriters.

I was anxious for show-and-tell with our project, especially as not many people were making their own records then. We first took the tape to a studio where I knew an engineer named Curt Allen, who agreed to make a reel-to-reel copy for us. Curt had to adjust the tape deck to accommodate our one-inch eight-track tape. It seemed that all the studios in Nashville had long before switched over to two-inch decks with sixteen or twenty-four tracks. We were obsolete on arrival. Overall, the response in Nashville was less than I might have hoped for. For starters, there was the matter of my folky predilection for minor keys and waltzes, which meant they were useless from a commercial point of view. Still, I was happy with what we had accomplished, and I secretly hoped that Mary would be impressed.

About this time, the ghost of Skinny Dennis began appearing. Townes and Susanna claimed he had visited them one night, causing a drink to disappear, a chair to move, and a door to slam. Dennis's claim to fame was his having been mentioned in Guy Clark's "L.A. Freeway," never mind that Guy was no longer speaking to him when he died. A soulful man, Dennis was attractive to women. He knew his heart was bad but was never one to take care of himself in the hope of living a few years longer. I wasn't entirely sure what to make of this latest story, but Dennis was much on my mind. I had decided to celebrate my upcoming birthday and the first anniversary of his demise together, and I began to set plans in motion. I booked a place called The Villager, on Twenty-First Street not far from our old house on Acklen.

On the 17th of March, we rehearsed with a band consisting of Rock on bass, Mickey White (who happened to show up in town) on guitar, Mary Bohanon playing fiddle, and me. Fred James offered the use of his PA. Rock designed posters, which we had printed and put up around Hillsboro Village and Music Row. I slipped one of these under Mary's door, not that she wouldn't already know.

Meanwhile, Bidey had an idea. "Come here, I want to show you something."

"What is it?"

"Follow me."

I followed Bidey outside. She led me around to the basement entrance by the side of the house, where there were stairs leading down. These were covered by a four-by-eight sheet of plywood painted gray. Over this, Bidey had painted a profile of Dennis in blue. She had captured him perfectly: his huge El Greco eyes and curling mustache. "You know, I think we can use this."

Bidey grinned, "That's exactly what I was thinking."

"We can make this into a backdrop behind the stage."

"Let's do it."

One of the things that had bonded Bidey and me together was our Catholic upbringing and education by priests and nuns. She had been trying to enlist me in a game of playing mass, where she was priest, and I was altar boy. She complained when I insisted I didn't know the Latin responses. "Come on," she said, "I know you were an altar boy."

"No I wasn't." I answered truthfully, though my mom had once hoped I might become one. But enough had rubbed off. Like mine, Bidey's roots were Irish. Rock was Italian and Skinny Dennis was Mexican, but we all shared this common background. Rock would have been the better choice to play altar boy as he had spent some years in the seminary where he had even composed a jazz mass. Now discussing stage decoration, we were of one accord. I first washed the board with a broom and soapy water before we took it across town and dragged it into the club. At Woolworth's I found a quantity of blue and white crepe paper, thumb tacks, and a bag of balloons. Back at the Villager the regulars, the daytime drinkers, looked on as we went to work. Some of them were still there twelve hours later.

The stage began to take shape with festoons of crepe paper all around Dennis, like high school prom decorations. When we got the PA set up, we decorated the speakers. Warming to our task, we wrapped the microphone stands in blue and white stripes, like maypoles in the colors of the Virgin. In a bar in Nashville, bastion of the born-again, where the real Industry was not hillbilly music but bible printing, we had created a pagan Catholic shrine. We stepped back and admired our work, sure that Skinny Dennis would have approved.

By now, word was out that something unusual was in the air. The bar was full that evening when we returned. I tapped on the microphone, "Ladies and gentlemen. I guess you might be wondering what we're doing here. Many of you knew Dennis Sanchez, who passed away a year ago tonight. As it happens, tonight is also my birthday and we're here to party."

And party we did, a rip-snorting barn-burner. My nights on the road opening for Townes had removed my uncertainty, and I played with a new confidence. I would never become a great guitar player but I had learned to keep rhythm, to find a groove and make it work for me. I could connect with an audience. Nearing completion of my first record, I felt like the course I had chosen was the right one. It felt good to have something coming together at a time when other things were falling apart.

Dave Olney played next. Then Fred James played some blues. Others took the stage and we got back up later. The place was crowded and smoky. We had tequila in a brown paper sack. Later, joints were going around, something unheard of in Nashville. But the cops never came to spoil our fun and the music didn't stopped until nearly three in the morning. It was too bad Rex was back in Texas and that Guy and Susanna didn't show up. Townes was out on the road somewhere. Late in the evening, Mary showed and invited me home with her. She said that she loved me and hated me at the same time. It was the last night we ever spent together, and we didn't make love.

Things took a turn for the worse a couple of days later, after I put Rock on a plane back to Houston. I wore out my welcome at Bidey's in a big hurry one afternoon when I tore a telephone receiver off the wall and slung it through a picture window. I smashed my image in the bathroom mirror and hurled a perfectly good portable typewriter to the floor. Bidey later said I threw a can of beans through the window, but I knew better. I knew better because I remembered what had triggered my rage; I had been talking on the phone with my wife.

Though I made arrangements to repair the damages, it was about this time I began to feel like a pariah, like my streak in Nashville had run out. Lovesick and drinking heavily, I hung on for another week or so, sleeping in a tent with a little dog named Snuffy John Lomax had given me. This was at Hugh Moffat's place, which had once been mine and Mary's. In the mornings, the neighborhood dogs would come around and pee on the tent, frolicking about until they had pulled up the stakes, and the walls collapsed around us. After a few days, I pulled up stakes myself and Snuffy and I started down the long road back to Texas.

A Lateral Move

Snuffy proved to be a good companion on the drive down. I drove straight through, stopping for gas and napping a couple of hours at a rest stop. Turning south past Texarkana and down through east Texas, we passed through Tyler, the town where I was born. Not feeling any vibrations, not even a hint, I drove on to my parent's house in Houston. "Home is where they have to take you in," my mother used to say, quoting Robert Frost. If it hadn't been for them, I would have been homeless. As it was, I was broke and clueless. There weren't enough gigs to keep me alive, and I couldn't think of any straight work I felt like doing. I began to think about going back to college and working toward a teaching certificate. Not for the first time, my folks bailed me out.

I decided to enroll in summer school and take some education courses at the University of Saint Thomas, where I had graduated ten years before. It was something different, I told myself. I had not darkened a schoolhouse door since the winter of '68 and '69, the year I taught school up in Michigan. Except for Peace Corps training, I hadn't attended classes myself since graduating back in '66, and I wondered what it might be like. Also I filed for—and was quickly granted—a divorce from Mary.

Then I learned Mickey had come back to Houston and was playing with Rex again. Starting as a duo, they soon teamed up with a drummer named Mike Edwards. Billing themselves as the Hemmer Ridge Mountain Boys, they played a number of my songs, along with Townes'. They did a lot of comedy with jokes, pratfalls, goofball parodies, and zany Rex Bell originals. They drew good crowds in Houston and Austin, where I drove up to hang out with them for a weekend. There, to my surprise, I ran into a dark haired beauty with a butterfly tattoo. I decided on the spot not to go back for a second semester of summer school.

Holly

The road from Texas to Nashville and back is burned in my mind, I've taken it so often. Whether we were fleeing or returning full of hope and determination to have another go at the music business, driving back to Houston for gigs at the Old Quarter, and later at Anderson Fair, hanging out at the beach and at Kerrville. I might have stayed on in Nashville but for the ghost of Skinny Dennis and the pain of losing Mary. I never realized I was moving back to Texas again until after the fact. Now in Austin, I was beginning to feel alive again. Mickey White was the first to comment on the fact that Holly and I were seeing each other. "Man, you got yourself a fox," he said. And I said to myself, "Yeah," trying to appear nonchalant, feeling inside a returning sense of man-pride and self-affirmation.

Holly had left her place on the lake and found a job in North Austin working for a credit union. She had an apartment within easy walking distance of Clarksville and Uncle Seymour's house. Here I found myself immersed in a world of bliss and fulfillment beyond my dreams or imagining. We are none of us born equal in this world, and just as there some people who excel in playing guitar or throwing a football, so there are a chosen few who excel in the art of love making. Holly was just such an exquisite creature, and she knew how to please.

Of course such a gift—as with any art—is not realized without considerable practice. There would be a price and there would come a reckoning. As Rex would put it, I was thinking with my dick. But that's what you do sometimes, because that is how a man's dick acts at nearly all times. Holly drove me to new heights of passion and arousal. She was every man's fantasy, and I, the big, sensitive song-poet, sure to cash in on fame and fortune. Moreover, I had found a way to close the door forever on the past; I slammed it shut and threw the bolt. I was rebounding like a shiny pinball, shot into a brand new game.

Holly had quit her previous job as a dancer. I had never hung out at topless bars and was just as happy she wasn't working those places anymore. But I was secretly thrilled. Now she danced for me at home. Weekends we went camping. I still had my old pup tent and we took off nearly every Friday for the Hill country: for Paleface Park, Enchanted Rock, or Pedernales Falls. Holly and I were married at the courthouse in Austin on July the ninth.

I settled into a song writing routine in the mornings, usually meeting Holly for a picnic lunch, and whiling away the afternoon hours in Clarksville while she was at back at work. Chito's girlfriend, Mary Ann, also worked days, so he and I passed the time drinking beer and listening to records. Around this time, Townes got in a bad way from drinking and checked into the hospital to dry out for a spell. Meanwhile, Unk, always a big eater, had begun to turn down food. He mentioned stomach pains, though nobody much noticed at first.

My idyll lasted about three weeks, before the inevitable occurred one morning as Holly was getting ready for work. "You know, you've got to get yourself some kind of job."

"I know, that's what I've been thinking."

"We can't make it on my salary alone."

"Don't worry, something will turn up." I knew from past experience that you don't just go out and find a job. More often, the job finds you. Sure enough, by the end of the month I found work with a plumber who had a contract to install showers in a public housing project over on the east side of I-35.

My new boss, whose name was Bill, explained my work to me. My job was to go in first and do the preparation. I was the point man. Armed with pipe wrenches and a powerful electric saber-saw, I would remove the fixtures and then cut out holes where the shower extension would go. I had a master key which allowed me access to hundreds of apartment units. Bill walked me through the first one, then I was on my own. I was set for a revelation of just how loathsome a day job can be.

I had seen hippie squalor, but not even Johnny Howard's trailer by the Intracoastal Canal, which relied on the occasional tide in lieu of a septic tank, had prepared me for the ground-in dirt and the hopelessness of project life. Sometimes the places were empty, often they were not. Almost all were cockroach infested. At each unit I approached key in hand and banged on the door, yelling "Plumber!" and then banging on the door again. If no one answered I went in anyway, half expecting to be shot. I turned aside as I pushed the door open, dodging a cascade of roaches that would be hiding in the sill.

Each evening I took long showers, scrubbing away the dirt and revulsion. It was a hot summer, but the lakes and rivers were cool where we camped and swam naked in the moonlight. Our nights at home were simple. We had no air conditioning, but there was a balcony and oak trees outside where we ate, listening to the cicadas. Then, in mid-August, Chito said he knew where we could get work in Louisiana as galley hands. I knew that offshore catering crews were not as well paid as regular hands, but, once again, I heard the siren call of the Gulf, the insistent pull of blue water fever. I was satiated, I was replete with sex, and I was ready to get out of the plumbing business.

Galley Hands

Tough and wiry, a good cook and storyteller, Chito was an old friend of Townes'. His father was a wealthy rancher who had adopted Chito as a baby. I heard that he had been disowned, though I never got the story straight and never asked. It may have had to do with Chito's drinking. I'm not sure what he had been drinking on the day we took off, but he passed out as soon as we left town.

   I was driving a Ford I inherited from my mom, a hard top two-door with a big engine. We headed out, making good time on Highway 71, Chito sleeping with his mouth open. He was still passed out at La Grange, where I drove down by the Colorado River to stretch my legs. I parked the car and walked down to the water's edge to skip a few stones. I returned to find Chito looking dazed, trying to wake up and collect himself. "Where are we?"

   "We're on our way to Louisiana, where did you think?"

   We drove on to Columbus, where we connected to I-10 that took us on into Houston. We stayed the night at my parents' home. Chito still looked rough the next morning. My mom had fixed some sandwiches to take with us. I hugged her goodbye in the driveway.

   "Are you sure he's all right?"

   "He's okay, Mom. He's just hung over."

   "Well, drive carefully." My folks were used to worrying about me, and with some reason. They seemed happy I was returning to work. They never said so, but I suspected they were not greatly impressed with the level of my success in the music business, not to mention the wisdom of my most recent marriage.

Chito and I drove on to Galveston and took the ferry across to Bolivar. We bought a six-pack at Zam's Famous For Nothing before heading up Highway 87 toward Port Arthur. Taking I-10 out of Houston would have been the quicker route, but I was always partial to the coast road. Besides, I wanted to check up on Johnny Howard. I asked around the docks and heard he was running another boat since the *Part Time* had run aground and broken up, just as it had threatened to do a couple of times before. It was getting dark by the time we joined up with I-10 at Winnie. We drove past Beaumont and Vidor, which, with Orange and Port Arthur, make up the Golden Triangle—redneck, Ku Klux Klan country—but also the birthplace of some great music. George Jones, Janis Joplin, Johnny and Edgar Winter all came from nearby. Past Orange, we crossed the Sabine River on another route that I had traversed more times than I could remember. Leaving the Interstate at Lafayette, we drove on into the wilds of South Louisiana.

At one point, we missed a turn and stopped at a roadhouse for directions. "Chito, run in and ask if we're on the right road to Houma."

He returned a few minutes later. "This way," he said as we pulled back onto the asphalt.

Driving on through the cane fields, we could see gas flares from time to time and the lights of a few houses. The potholed road kept twisting until I lost all sense of direction. I was getting tired but didn't offer to let Chito drive. We stopped again to ask directions at another roadside bar. I had the feeling that if we both went in we would want to have a drink and we'd never get out of there. You could get yourself killed in South Louisiana, particularly if you came from somewhere else. Once again, Chito went in for directions and we took off down the road. It was getting on toward midnight when I began losing patience. "Chito, I think we're going in circles."

"Just keep going."

The lights of another roadside joint appeared, and I pulled off again. I began to suspect Chito was getting himself a shot every time we stopped. It was just the kind of trick Townes would pull. I realized we had arrived back at the first place we stopped. "Goddamit, Chito, we've already been here asking for directions."

Chito exploded into laughter. "Hell, I know that, we passed the same dead skunk in the road three times."

We never found the road to Houma that night, but found a sixteen dollar room in the little town of Kaplin and turned in. The next morning, we made our way to Houma with no trouble and started making the rounds of various catering companies that serviced the offshore fields. We lucked out at the third place we tried and signed up. Our crew change would come the following evening.

Chito knew of a run-down hotel where we were able to get a room. The place was full of galley hands and cooks trying to hire on with one of the companies. Regular oilfield hands always considered the galley help to be several rungs below them on the social ladder. According to conventional wisdom, the galley folk were all wine-heads, and from the looks of the guys hanging around the hotel, the oil fielders were right.

We had plenty of time to wander around Houma, though there wasn't a great deal to see. I pawned a shotgun I had in the trunk for fifteen dollars at a bar down the street and brought a six-pack up to the room. Chito was stretched out, reading.

"Care for a beer?"

"No thanks." Chito went back his book. As much as he drank, he didn't appear to have any trouble sobering up when he put his mind to it.

The hotel was shabby, but our room was clean and nicely situated on a corner overlooking a small park. I had found a book of my own to read, *The Great Train Robbery*. After a while, I lit up one of my stash of joints, which set my heart to trembling and my brain singing with memories of all those other days and nights out on the Gulf. The room was warm, but a ceiling fan kept the air moving. Some night birds were holding forth from different sides of the park. An occasional car or truck went by. I heard someone cough down on the sidewalk.

We stayed the next day as long as we could, leaving the hotel around noon. We wandered around for a few hours and slept that night on the floor of the dispatcher's office at the heliport. We boarded a chopper for the rig just after daylight and lifted off. Chito, who was afraid of flying, never looked up from his book as we rose up over the swamps and headed towards open water.

It was an hour's flight before we set down on rig PO-17, about a hundred miles out. One of the platform variety, it was a permanent structure rising on steel columns anchored to the sea floor. Once on board, we went straight to work changing sheets for the incoming crew. I would rather have been working outside, but it beat the hell out of installing showers in the projects back in Austin.

But of course, we weren't aboard the rig three days before a horny attack set in. So much for my sense of satiation. Chito had finished his novel and come across a stash of well-thumbed fuck-books, but I resisted borrowing one at first. Just like all the rigs and boats I had worked on, these made up the main source of reading material on the PO-17. Serious readers favored Louis L'Amor westerns and, more rarely, espionage-adventure novels. Once, I ran across a book on the teachings of Gurdijeff, but he was a long way from home. This time I had found myself a Zane Grey novel.

"I don't like him," opined one of the older guys who happened to walk by.

"Why's that?"

"He puts in too damn much scenery."

"Really, what makes you say that?"

"I like it when they keep the action going, I don't like a bunch of talk about scenery."

By now we had settled into our routine of making beds,

sweeping and mopping floors, and scrubbing and disinfecting the toilets and showers. When we finished with our cleaning chores, we helped the cook in the galley. The place was spotlessly clean and air conditioned. Outside was a blinding white-hot world of sweat, noise, and steel. One day, a very frightened lady photographer came aboard. Apparently, the height unnerved her, for she clung to the wall, looking fearfully down through the grating to the waves heaving far below. The tool pusher who was showing her around made light of her anxiety. "It doesn't matter if you fall ten feet or a hundred, ma'am. The barracudas will get you anyway."

One night, the off-duty drilling crew caught a shark, a big one measuring over eight feet. They brought him in on a quarter-inch nylon line using a Clorox jug as a float. It took four or five men to haul it in. They killed it with a fire axe and, after admiring their work, dropped the carcass back into the Gulf.

PO-17 changed crews on a seven-and-seven basis. Some of the companies went fourteen-and-seven. One of the rigs we worked on in the Bahamas had us working twenty-and-ten. That's too damn long for twelve-hour days that would often run three or four hours overtime. The best deal was working alternate weeks, provided you didn't have to drive too far. With crew change coming, Chito elected to stay on and pull an extra hitch. The company asked me to stay on, but I had a gig the next weekend at the Gangplank in Galveston. Holly was coming down from Austin to meet me.

On my last night, I took a cup of coffee from the galley and a joint outside to a place on the handrail where I could see anyone coming. While I smoked and watched the lights out on the water, I didn't fear discovery as the breeze carried the smoke away. You would have to have been very close to tell I was not smoking a "ready-roll" of ordinary tobacco. Later in my bunk, I consulted the pages of one of the fuck-books I had broken down and borrowed from Chito. The line from a Jackson Browne song came into my head, "Honey, let me introduce you to my redneck friend." I fell asleep thinking of a dark haired beauty with a butterfly tattoo.

Several weeks passed before I saw Chito again, and that was back in Austin. He had stayed on his extra hitch, and by the time I got back offshore he was gone. Siting in the heliport waiting for my flight, I talked with a skinny guy with a hard face and prison tattoos who asked "Are you going to PO-17?"

"Yeah, this is my second hitch."

"Are you roughnecking?"

"No, I'm working as a galley hand."

"A galley hand!" He didn't bother to mask his derision.

I smarted from the slight. A few days later, I was out on deck taking a break and watching the action where they were beginning to run casing, the pipe that goes into the hole first to keep the walls of the well from caving in. The crane operator had just picked up a load and was booming over towards the v-door, when I noticed the skinny roustabout standing underneath looking confused at the shouts and whistles coming this way. "Look out, you fucking worm," I yelled, joining the others. "Worm" is oilfield slang for greenhorn. One of the first things I had learned some fifteen years before was never to stand under a crane load. Not for the first time, the notion came to me that I should have been outside in the fresh air making good money with the real men whose beds I made, whose plates I scraped and washed, and whose greasy boot tracks I mopped from the galley floor.

Despite my resolution, I stayed on four another hitch at the end of my seven days, just as Chito had done two weeks before. The days slipped by without further incident. You could always tell the night before crew change, when the men became talkative with horseplay and singing in the shower.

"Hey Freddy, what are you gonna do when you get home?"

"I'm gonna sit down with a tub of ice cold beer and crack one open."

"Yeah man, I heard that."

"Then I'm gonna suck my old lady's pussy 'til her eyeballs cave in."

"Yahooo, I heard that!"

That evening I watched the sunset from the rail. Stiff breeze and white capped seas, a hint of fall in the air. The declining sun was a hot blaze of gold, lighting up the sky behind dark banks of swollen cloud. I could see three rigs working to the south and west, tow platforms, and a drill ship. In a fantasy, I imagined tumbleweeds out in the Gulf, rolling across the deck. In the waning light, the Gulf turned from deep blue to black as the sun edged lower, highlighting cloud shapes of swans and dragons. Surely there were only so many sunsets to be observed in a lifetime. The sun slipped below the horizon, turning the clouds to embers. The first star appeared, and I made my wish. Bring me home safely to my darling. Make the hours fly.

Farewell Uncle Seymour

September was nearly gone when I got back to Austin, where I learned that Uncle Seymour had been diagnosed with cancer and wasn't going to get any better. In *Heartworn Highways*, you can see him as he used to look; the film shows Unk hanging out on his front porch philosophizing with Townes, who is playing a song on the guitar. In the midst of a discussion about whiskey, Seymour tells him, "Townes, the Lord made whiskey for man to enjoy, but he never intended for him to drink a whole barrel of it."

I heard that he had lost a lot of weight, but I wasn't ready for the way Unk had changed when I went to visit him at a nursing home over on the east side of I-35. What used to be a big man with an appetite to match, that day Seymour looked as if he had simply quit eating. The nursing home didn't feel so much like a haven for old age so much as a place where you went to die: a charnel house by the Ganges, the penultimate destination. In anticipation of Halloween, someone had decorated the halls with strings of orange and black crepe paper ribbons and cut out skeletons. Banshee howling came from a room down the hall, and someone in delirium began hollering, "Police! Police! I know it's the police!"

Two elderly black men in suits were sitting by Seymour when I walked in, deacons from the Free Home Baptist Church in Clarksville. I shook hands with them. They were polite but ill at ease. Seymour scowled at them balefully. I guessed there had never been much love lost between them and Seymour, a self-appointed preacher, particularly after he'd had a couple of drinks.

Seymour opened up a bit after they left. He was lucid but weak. "Richard, would you help me. I'm going to try to go to the bathroom in that pan there under the bed."

"Sure, Unk." I set the pan on the floor away from the bed and helped raise him up. He was wearing a lose flannel gown, which he bunched up as I lowered him down over the pan. I could hold him up easily. He weighed less than a sack of drilling mud, about forty kilos. After a time, I lifted him up and sat him back down on the bed.

"Richard, did I do anything?"

I glanced down at the bedpan. "No, Unk, you didn't do nothing." It seemed that Seymour was starving himself rather than waiting on the cancer.

"I didn't do nothing?"

"You've got to eat before you can shit, Unk. I don't think you've been eating."

"I know that, Richard."

"You better get some rest, Unk. I'll come back and see you."

Seymour Washington could not have known that my mom's father, Jim Maloney, born in Ireland, and his brother, Patrick, born in Kansas, were both railroad men. Gramps had been conducting well into his sixties on a run that took him from Albuquerque, up over Raton Pass, and north to La Junta, Colorado. Seymour had been a blacksmith, but his last words to me called up images of steam trains and days that are no more, of things I had known in my own time, now gone or swiftly passing. "Richard, this old engine's going to the roundhouse."

"So long, Unk. I'll be back."

But that was the last I ever saw of Seymour Washington. I left the nursing home with its orange and black streamers and dancing skeletons and walked out into the bright Austin sunshine.

Holly and I drove down to Galveston the next weekend for a gig, returning Sunday evening. A couple of days later, there was a benefit for Seymour at the Soap Creek Saloon. The money would go to fix up his house with indoor plumbing so that a nurse could stay there and look after him. As I remember, the old Soap Creek Saloon was situated on top of a hill at the back of a rough, unpaved parking lot. I went on early. Townes had flown in from Nashville but arrived too drunk to play. He broke a string right away, and I loaned him my guitar. He sat before the microphone and told jokes. Titters ran through the audience. Then someone handed me an announcement to read, saying that Seymour's house would be fitted with hot water and an indoor toilet free of charge. We left the stage to scattered applause as a band called Greasy Wheels began setting up and tuning. They played a long set that got everybody up dancing.

Someone told me later that night that Seymour had refused medication and gone into delirium, asking for liver and onions, barbecue, and pumpkin pie. The last thing I remember was leaving the parking lot with Chito and a guy named Pussycat. JJ Wanker had elected to ride on the roof of the car while Pussycat careened through the potholed parking lot trying his best to dislodge him. JJ clung to the roof like a remora to a shark. As for Unk, he never made it out of the nursing home. He didn't need indoor plumbing any more than he needed that bedpan.

Daddy Bill

Holly had been telling me about Daddy Bill, her real father, who once owned a marina on Lake Livingston but had chucked it all for a fishing camp on the Trinity River bottom near the town of Crockett. We drove up to see him one weekend, and since we knew Bill didn't have a phone down at the camp, we asked for directions at a café on the town square. We learned that he was no longer living on the river, but had rented a place nearby and had a phone after all. We followed his directions and met him at the little community of Austonio.

Bill was stocky and deeply tanned, except for his bald head, which was white from always being under a cap. He had a twinkle in his eye and a ready laugh, and I took a liking to him right away. He was glad to see Holly, whom he hadn't seen in several years. She introduced me as a great songwriter, sure to become successful. Bill introduced us to his new wife, Vera, and that quickly we all became family. "Y'all follow us to the house." he said, "We've got plenty of room."

My first view of the camp the next day corroborated my favorable impression of my new father-in-law. Ramshackle and homemade, situated on a bluff overlooking the river, it consisted of two rooms in the form of a T. On the back wall hung the antlers of fifteen or twenty deer. The kitchen had a wood-burning stove for heat and a Coleman propane stove for cooing, with pots and pans hanging from nails. There was no electricity. Outside, an artesian well ran a two-inch stream into a holding tank that exited into the river. A lean-to shed on the side of the house was filled with all manner of traps and nets, old lanterns, gas cans, and outboard motor parts. At the front, parallel to the two-track road, was a garden. On the other side, facing the river was a long bench. "This is the meditation bench," Bill said, "where you can just sit and watch the river."

Bill brought some cold beers from a cooler in the back of his truck, and we looked over the river running swift and muddy, about thirty yards across. "How's the fishing?" I asked.

He looked at me with a twinkle, an almost conspiratorial wink. "Man, that river is full of fish. There's more fish in there than you can imagine."

"Looks like you've got a few deer around here too."

"We've got deer, ducks, quail, raccoons, bobcats. You name it and you'll find it down here on the bottom."

I didn't need to hear more. Holly and I made arrangements to come back the following weekend for the opening of deer season. A far cry from the saltwater world I was used to, Bill's camp seemed to promise a treasure of hunting and fishing opportunity and new country to explore. Holly's mother and stepfather lived in the suburbs in North Austin, where her younger half-sisters and brother went to high school and listened to Peter Frampton records. But Daddy Bill, a free spirit who lived by hunting and fishing and trapping down on the river, was my kind of guy.

I didn't see a deer when we returned in late November, when Bill had invited us to come back and stay at the camp as long as we liked. A couple of weeks later we did. Holly quit her job at the credit union. We picked up Snuffy, who had been staying at my folks' house in Houston. Bill had a lot of dogs. A line from Jesse Winchester's song "Mississippi You're On My Mind" goes a ways toward describing Bill's collection of hounds that lived off fish heads and whatever they could scrounge. "And the dogs, my God, they're hungry all the time." I was initially worried about Snuffy being suddenly thrust into this world, but he seemed to thrive on it.

It didn't cost much, living down at the camp. Holly signed up for unemployment in Crockett and got a check right away. We drove to Houston and Galveston for weekend gigs. I helped Bill run his nets, hooped contrivances anchored in the current. Swimming upstream, the fish entered through a series of small holes and, once there, couldn't turn around and swim back out. Bill sold his fish at a market just outside of Crockett. He was right about the Trinity River. Always muddy and fluctuating according to the rains, it wasn't pretty to look at, but it held a world of fish: white bass, and catfish, both channel and flathead; the natives called them Opelousas and the fish grew up to five feet long and as big around as your leg. There were also drum and big carp in the river, which we threw back or saved for the dogs. Bill was a great believer in fish. He claimed to have raised hogs that turned out as pretty as any he'd ever seen, exclusively on fish.

Besides fish, we had duck and venison. Bill was the best wing-shot I ever saw, and I kept a freezer full of game at the farmhouse where he and Vera lived. In the evenings, we used to sit around while I played guitar. Bill didn't play an instrument but he loved to sing after he had warmed up with a few beers. The Kenny Rogers hit "Lucille" was one of his favorites. He told us that Rogers, whose family came from Crockett, had tried to buy a color television at a local store on credit and was turned down right before the song hit.

"Is that really true?"

"Gospel."

"I guess he could go back and buy the whole store now."

I believed Bill's story. I still thought I was going to write my own hit song, though what made me think this confounds me now. I wasn't really in the music business anymore, if I ever had been. I was running away. From love gone bad and Skinny Dennis and now Uncle Seymour. I was still writing songs, though I never recorded any I penned during this time. One really sad one was called "Going to the Roundhouse" after Unk's last words to me. Around this time, the Outlaw movement in Country music was taking off with Willie and Waylon and the Boys. Among them was the blustery megalomaniac and ex-convict who billed himself as the Mysterious Rhinestone Cowboy, a.k.a. David Allan Coe. I hadn't seen any royalty money from "Piece of Wood and Steel" yet, but I did hear David was going around the country claiming it as his own song.

It rained a lot that winter, and we were often isolated for days at a time when the two-track down to the river became impassable mud. On warm days, we sat on the meditation bench and practiced shooting at bottles floating down the river. Taking after her dad, Holly was a damned good shot. There was never a shortage of targets, and I wondered if they had floated all the way down from Dallas.

I was beginning to learn other things about Holly. For one, I was becoming immune to her charms in a way I had never been with Mary. Her efforts to tempt me, her lascivious flirtations, caused me to smile as much as they inspired ardor. Also, she was beginning to reveal more of her past. I didn't mind that she had been a topless dancer, but I was beginning to see how it had affected her attitude. Not counting stints on boats and drilling rigs, I had gone straight from college to the Peace Corps to my years as a folksinger. I never had the money to hand out in titty bars. Now I was beginning to see how Holly had been spoiled by the easy money, the perks, and the attention. She was now discovering that life with me was not all that she had imagined. While Townes, even in those days, was pulling in two hundred dollars or more a night, I was lucky to make fifty. I hoped the release of my first record would change things, but I didn't know where the money was going to come from to finish it.

"Don't you think it's about time you found a job?"

"Yeah, I know."

"We can't just hang out on the river forever."

"Maybe I can find something in Crockett."

"We can't live on my unemployment."

"I know." Holly was right. Not that I wasn't starting to think she was acting a little crazy. Maybe she was bored. There wasn't any question that I loved her. She was damned good-looking, and I liked being seen with her. As yet, we had not been away from each other long enough to test her fidelity. A quote in my journal taken from *Best Quotations* prophesized the drift of events, like the pull of the Trinity River headed to the Gulf:

> *Thus grief still treads upon the heels of pleasure*
> *Married in haste we may repent at leisure.*

In January, Holly told me she was late with her period. We had not discussed having children and I was quietly thankful when she miscarried the following month. In February, JJ Wanker showed up at the camp, ostensibly to play some music, but he never got his Telecaster out of the case. Not that there was any place to plug it in. About this time, I killed an eight-point buck, dropping it cleanly with one shot through the neck with Bill's .22 magnum. Deer season was over, but I took him for food, not for sport. One of the antlers came off as I was dragging it away.

We left Bill's camp on the Trinity sometime in early March of 1977. We may have gone back up to Austin for a few days, but we were back in Houston at Anderson Fair for my birthday on the nineteenth, the second anniversary of Skinny Dennis' death.

Meanwhile, my father had a friend who put in a word for me with a drilling company that had a big semi-submersible rig working out of Freeport. Holly and I drove down to the office where I filled out an application and took a physical. I was hired on as a maintenance roustabout. Holly seemed pleased about my decision to return to real work. I was thirty-five and it was time to quit playing Huckleberry Finn. Holly and I found a place in Galveston, a clean second-floor efficiency apartment just a few blocks from the beach.

Rig Logs

For some reason, we changed crews by work boat on my first hitch back offshore, leaving the dock at Freeport about ten in the evening on March 29th. I slept most of the trip out on a pile of slightly damp life preservers. Once on board, I found my duties would be those of a maintenance roustabout: chipping and painting. Owned by a Dutch-American consortium, *Sedneth I* had lots of deck space. The hands seemed friendly, if a little younger than I remembered, and I felt at home right away. I resolved to keep up with my journal and make the best of things. A line from a John Lennon song went through my head, "A working class hero is something to be."

It was foggy the first day of my first tour as I reacquainted myself with the sights, smells, and sounds of an offshore drilling rig. *Sedneth I* was an island of steel, floating on pontoons and heaving slowly, secured by gigantic winches at each corner with cable as thick as a man's forearm.

Colors: Yellow for handrails and ladders, black for winches, red for fire extinguishers, axes, and fire-hose boxes, blue for mud-pumps. Green was the color of the drill collars, the extra heavy joints of pipe that went down in the hole first. Decks and bulkheads were battleship gray, while the walls of the crew's quarters were white. Skies were full of clouds ranging from white to rain-laden gray to the blue sky between them and the Gulf below, white-capped in fresh weather. And there was the sun, a fierce molten ball of orange at sunrise and again come evening, which became softer as the heat let go. And the brows, grease and pipe dope with a sheen like big tree-roaches, the wash of rust stains on a bulkhead wall, and the crew-hand Fat Boy's belly, bigger than any watermelon.

Smells: Sweat and hot sun on skin and metal, fresh paint, diesel exhaust, the acrid, sizzling smoke from arc-welding rods, antiseptic pine-soap smell in the hallways, food cooking in the galley.

Sounds: The roar of engines, the cranes and the big generating plant, the hiss of compressed air that powered the winches and hand tools, the whine of grinders and clatter of needle guns, the clang and clash of iron, the train sounds from up on the rotary drill floor, and the thumping *hum* of the mud pumps that washed up the cuttings and stabilized the pressure of the earth itself. In the quarters you could hear shouts in the halls, a clatter of plastic plates and silverware in the galley, the roar of air-conditioning through the ducts, the cricket chirp of vibrating locker doors, the water splashing in the showers, the flush of toilets, and squeak and slam of paper-towel dispensers, the whir of dryers in the laundry room, and Ping-Pong being played in the auxiliary room.

March 31st came up cool and foggy. Fat Boy (sometimes called Tiny) and I worked chipping and scraping under the V-door ramp with needle-guns and grinders, rust and paint flakes swirling all around us. Then we applied red lead-primer paint. Humming tunes that came and went, I tried to maintain just the right mental stance, to remind myself why I was there. Later, I finished reading *The Boys From Brazil*. I had another ready to start, *The Californios* by Louis L'Amour, lots of action and not too much scenery, thanks.

April Fool's Day: Nice weather with blue skies and a fresh breeze, the Gulf blue and white-capped. Helicopters coming and going. Another day chipping and painting. I burned my thigh from having a rag soaked in paint thinner in my pocket. I settled into a routine, my mind drifting away to Holly and life ashore. I felt strong, though somewhat stiff and achy.

April 2nd: Another day of buffing, laying down primer, painting it over. A ladder slipped on me in the morning. Luckily, I had it tied off at the top. I clung to it, bruising my arm. Later, a work boat came. Saw three porpoises.

April 3rd: Sunday. I spent the morning cleaning and painting up on the helicopter deck. Took off my shirt and got a little sunburn. Safety meeting after lunch. Back outside, singing snatches of songs coming from nowhere. Missing Holly already. Later, guys yelling and singing in the showers. Tired. No problem keeping up with my work, but I can tell I ain't twenty-one anymore. Big deal. Somehow, the hours passed. Hoping to come up with a song.

April 4th: A squally morning with thundershowers, later clearing with high thin clouds. Later still, a big yellow moon. Toothache, crown loose. Seven days gone.

April 5th: Talking blues: I've been playing this old guitar here/ Closing in on fourteen years/ Never made much money but I get by/ Folks put me up and get me high/ Living off dreams and beans and dope/ I sure got tired of being broke/ Thought I'd try my luck as a working man/ Make an honest living with my own two hands/ Fix my truck, buy my wife a dress/ Pay a regular share to the IRS/ I had a friend who said he'll get me a gig/ Working offshore on a big oil rig/ Way out in the Gulf of Mexico/ I said Far Out when do we go? / He said crew change is Tuesday/ I said Out of Sight!/ He said you better believe you got that right/ It's ninety miles out of Freeport in 227 feet of water.

April 6th: Light wind out of the southeast. Still, brassy sea. Hot. The barge captain put us on a painting job at twenty minutes 'til quitting time. Paul, the maintenance foreman, and Fat Boy went out after dinner to finish the job, a small patch of deck. Took them all of ten minutes. Barge captain enjoying weird power games. Five days left 'til crew change.

April 7th: This evening finished *Volume II* of John Jake's *Bicentennial* Series, lots of swashbuckling history. Things had gotten weird earlier at day's finish when we had to go back outside after dinner and paint a section of deck with the whole crew under threat of being fired. The barge captain said we get no overtime pay for this. I think it best to keep my mouth shut, but fuck him anyway.

April 8th: Another long day. Finally finished the helicopter deck. Sunburned. Worked two hours overtime after dinner. Wind out of the west, cloudy after two days of blue skies. Tired, the urge to sleep stronger than my wish to stay up and read and write, steal an hour for myself.

April 9th: Two more days to go. Wrote Townes a letter. Worked overtime the last three evenings.

April 10th: Easter Sunday. One more day to go. Two more wake-ups. Hope the weather holds fair so the choppers can fly. Lord, keep the fog away. Glad this hitch is almost over. Looks like I'll be promoted to regular roustabout before long, maybe even roughneck. Thoughts of Holly. Gig at The Gangplank next weekend.

April 11th: End of hitch! Going home tomorrow on the last flight.

April 12th: Shouts and slamming locker doors. *Whup, whup, whup,* the chopper arriving with a fresh crew ready to go on tour, a subdued lot compared to the men going home. Climbing the steel steps in our sneakers and cowboy boots, donning our life jackets for the ride to the beach. Aboard and strapped in, the chopper lifts off the deck, gaining altitude, *Sedneth I* beneath us with the derrick and pipe racks, the anchor winches all clearly visible down below, the white-capped seas. Passing more rigs and shrimp boats anchored up for the day. The engine noisy, hypnotic. The men reading, napping, or lost in thought. A line of surf appearing below, the Texas coast. Dropping altitude, we pass over the Intracoastal Canal, the docks and chemical refineries, and set down at the heliport.

Holly was there to meet me at the parking lot. I felt proud knowing the other men wouldn't help but notice what a good looker she was. I got in the car and kissed her, and we headed back towards Galveston. She was wearing a sun dress which she let ride up her thighs. She wasn't wearing any underwear. At a convenience store, I ran in and bought an ice cold six-pack and cracked one open as we passed over the Brazos River where I had once run in during a Norther with Bud and Johnny Howard. We passed the Dow Chemical plants, Surfside, and the Jesus is Lord Surf Shop, turning left on the beach road that leads over San Luis Pass to the Island. I reached over and touched her, and she parted her legs to let me explore, giving off small shudders of ecstasy and the promise of more to come.

The Key

If the long days aboard the rig crawled by, the days and nights ashore fairly flew. It was a happy time. Situated over a row of shops, our apartment overlooked a palm-lined boulevard. It was clean and uncluttered, since we had not had much time to collect stuff. We arose early on Tuesday, April 18th, to drive to the heliport at Freeport. There is a saying in the offshore oil patch which goes, "You can't catch up, but you can get even." By ten in the morning, I was back on board *Sedneth I*, not caught up, but even.

Jesse Levy, the barge engineer, was a thin, nervous fellow with the demeanor of a college man cast among a crew of good old boy southern rednecks. Fat Boy was also an anomaly, not because he was black—which by 1977 was no longer unusual offshore—but because of his enormous girth. He was almost too big to get around on a drilling rig. But Tiny just happened to come from the same town as the tool pusher and did the driving for him on crew-change days. We were working together painting the control room of the starboard anchor winch when Jesse came snooping around to check on us.

"Richard, you like eating pussy, don't you?" Tiny never stopped painting.

"Yeah, I like to eat pussy. I can go down on it pretty good when I'm drunk."

"You know what they say, don't you?" Tiny reached out and caught a dribble of paint where it had started to run.

"Yeah, I know what they say."

"Once you get past the smell, you got it licked."

"I heard that."

Jesse Levy made a hasty retreat. Thirty-eight years old and still a virgin, dirty talk would always send him packing.

On the first evening back offshore, there was a fresh westerly wind with horizontal banks of cloud, slate to marble.

We fast forward through those numbing days. Days of toil and boredom alleviated by moments of awesome beauty and, occasionally, great danger. Fat Boy and I spent several days working down in the starboard pump room, fifty feet below sea level, chipping paint and fighting claustrophobia, the machine gun clattering of needle guns and the bilge swishing and gurgling beneath us. Then I was promoted to regular roustabout, which paid the same but gave me a wider range of tasks and meant I was no longer at the bottom of the heap. I was secretly considering the possibility of roughnecking up on the drill floor, where the real action took place.

Death touched my shoulder one day, just a nudge, a cold premonition on a warm afternoon, real, like the whiff of a passing bullet. I was perched with a needle gun on one of the giant anchor winches some fifteen feet above the catwalk when suddenly the great wheel began to shudder and move, paying out cable as thick as a man's forearm. With no choice but to leap or be crushed, I jumped. The trajectory of my fall landed me on the catwalk while my hard hat went sailing overboard. Trembling with adrenaline, I watched it float for a minute, then fill with water and sink beneath the waves. The incident was quickly forgotten as the men went back to work. It was not my first close call offshore, simply one of the more dramatic ones.

The days followed one upon another and soon I was back on the Island. Holly had discussed taking up macramé or maybe going back to school, but it didn't look like she had made any moves.

"Did you go by the community college and pick up a class schedule?"

"No, not yet."

"What about a job?"

"I'm not ready to go back to work just yet."

I could understand her point but I was trying to make one of my own. "Well, you've got to do something. You can't just be sitting here while I'm working like a dog, risking my life offshore."

Holy looked at me with wide round eyes that suggested much reveled nothing. It seemed I never understood the women I became involved with beyond giving in to fascination, which became a surging undertow of chemistry over which I had no control. We forgot our conversation as we lay back and lapsed into lazy foreplay.

Later that afternoon, when we were getting ready to go out I found a key on the dresser and idly tried it in the door. "What's this key for?" I asked when Holly came out of the bathroom.

"I don't know."

"I tried it in the door and it doesn't fit."

"It's not mine."

"Well, it doesn't belong to me."

Nothing more was said of the key, which was by itself with no chain or ring. I tossed it back on the dresser and we went out the door. Time would reveal that Holly had been far from idle during my absence, but I was preoccupied with business to do up in Houston where, at long last, my record had entered the final stages of production.

Kerrville

An ice water fight broke out in the showers the second night of my fifth hitch. The next evening, a roughneck got hurt and had to be evacuated by helicopter. By now I was feeling in pretty good condition, but I couldn't help but notice that I didn't have the speed and agility of my new co-workers, most of them fifteen years my junior. One afternoon I jammed my thumb, not seriously, but enough to start me wondering. You noticed a lot of missing digits on a drilling rig, particularly among the older hands. Billy Joe Shaver was doing okay with his music career despite having lost the fingers of his right hand in the sawmill accident, but it wasn't something I wanted to set myself up for.

Each day on board brought a new test of my ability to stay good natured and keep a positive attitude. There was plenty of time for introspection in a twelve-hour day. I always had a song going, a running soundtrack in my mind. I began to think about going back to shrimping as an alternative to roughnecking. It was every bit as dangerous, but at least I wouldn't have some creep like Jesse Levy looking over my shoulder all the time. As for Holly, I had talked to her about the possibility of putting some money down on a double-wide in Bolivar, but found her unreceptive to the idea. "No way," she said.

"We could save some money."

"I don't want to live in a trailer."

"We can't afford a real house now. At least we won't be throwing money away on rent."

"I don't want to live on Bolivar, it's too isolated."

I didn't pursue the issue. I could see her point. I figured the only solution was to stick it out on the rig as long as I could and see what happened. The test pressing for my record had come back from the plant in Louisiana, and we were expecting delivery in a couple of weeks. In the meantime, another Kerrville Folk Festival was coming up, and we had made plans to go during my off week.

I had been hanging out at Kerrville ever since the first festival was held at the fairgrounds with an evening concert at the high-school auditorium. This was in '71, before I moved to Nashville, a year or two before it moved to Quiet Valley Ranch. I remember sitting across the aisle from a beaming Lyndon Johnson, who had come with an entourage of family and Secret Service. Kenneth Threadgill was on stage playing Jimmie Rodgers, and Lyndon— who looked like he might have had a drink or two—was enjoying himself immensely. The others were not enjoying themselves quite so much. I remember catching Lyndon's eye, and in that instant he did not have the look of a man with blood on his hands. Sending so many boys to Vietnam had taken the luster off the Great Society, but it did not preclude Lyndon from having a good time. He was the second president I had seen close up. Long before on a bitterly cold morning, on N Street in Georgetown, I had watched from across the street as JFK and Jackie got into a limo and rode off to his inauguration.

I returned often to Kerrville in the years following, beginning with the trip with Mary and Skinny Dennis when we had driven straight through to Austin. Mary had freaked out when I started cutting cross-country on farm roads at night. It was her first trip to Texas, excluding the one she made with Rodney. Most of what I remember from this trip was hanging out, partying with Guy and Susanna Clark, and Jerry Jeff Walker. I remember a terrible argument with Mary in a motel room in Fredericksburg, and I remember that Denis got so eaten up with chiggers he moaned all the way back to Tennessee. I remembered other times, including the year when it rained and JJ Wanker repeatedly stuck in the

Blue Unit in the mud until he got himself banned for life.

Holly and I drove to Kerrville in her Toyota. On the way, I noticed she was ignoring my sexual overtures, but I wasn't greatly worried. I had a feeling that something was not quite right, but I was anxious to get the Festival. I was happy for the one thing she had given me. She had cut the cord forever between me and Mary.

We hadn't made any camping arrangements beyond bringing a cooler and my old pup tent. Nor did I see much of Holly after first setting it up. Everyone was in party mode, and at first I didn't notice what was going on. Kerrville was the kind of place where we stayed up and partied until we fell out. The festival promoter, Rod Kennedy, always made a pointed effort to keep his event from becoming a Texas Woodstock, denouncing drugs at every opportunity. But there were still plenty around, mainly of the organic, recreational variety. The nightly campfires were redolent with the sweet smell of burning marijuana.

There were other diversions, as well-the thrill of new encounters, of tent floor and camper shell seductions under a Hill Country moon. A few weeks earlier, Rex had introduced me to a school teacher he was dating, Angie, a slim, quiet girl from Galveston who had come to one of his gigs. "She's nice," I said.

"I thought you'd like her. You two should get together."

"Rex, you're forgetting I'm married."

"That's right. You are, aren't you?"

It took me awhile before I figured Rex was trying to protect me from getting hurt again but didn't want to spill the beans. A couple of days later, I found myself emerging from a tent with his schoolteacher only to be confronted with Holly, who wore an expression of mock outrage. She had caught me dead to rights. But time would reveal I was in fact the cuckold, and the cuckoldry had been going on for some time.

Changing Partners

On the 30th of May, I was back offshore. On the 5th of June, a Sunday, we held a safety meeting, followed by an abandon-ship drill. Sometime in the night there came a violent pounding on the door and shouts in the hall. It was déjà vu, "Everybody up! We're evacuating!"

"Aw shit, another drill."

"No man, this ain't no fucking drill. The well's done blowed out!"

We hurriedly donned clothes and life jackets. I grabbed my Martin, hoping there would be room for it. Outside, we were met by a terrifying roar as a column of natural gas shot straight through the drill floor, up to the crown of the derrick. We watched, spellbound, knowing one spark could blow us to smithereens and turn the whole rig into a fireball. We waited for orders to climb into the lifeboats. These were not lifeboats at all but looked like flying saucers. Nobody was making a move to climb in. Just then the blowout preventer kicked in and closed off the well. We filed back inside as the roaring subsided, the men shaking their heads and muttering.

"Jesus, that was a close one."

"Yeah, I thought we were goners."

The next morning, we discovered the blowout had pushed all the drilling mud out of the hole, and we spent several hours washing down the rig with saltwater fire hoses. The danger of the previous night forgotten, we made horseplay, squirting one another in the powerful, stinging blast.

Then on June 14th, after a week ashore, we took off from Freeport in a driving rainstorm. Gaining altitude and heading out over the water, our visibility was reduced to nothing as we were buffeted by violent gusts of wind. About thirty minutes out, a flash of lighting knocked out the radio. The pilot took the chopper down just over the water, passing over a work boat. Everyone was smoking while one of the cooks, a Cajun lady, began fingering her rosary. Once again, I felt a cold chill as a jack-up rig appeared before us. The pipe racks just below and the V-door ramp leading up to the drill floor rushed toward us as the pilot pulled away sharply away. We had missed certain death by an instant.

There was no laughing or joking when we set down on our own rig a few minutes later, took our bags out, and walked down to the crew's quarters. The pilot had seen his own death coming. He poured a cup of coffee and sat by himself in the galley. He stared at his coffee a long time, though there was a crew going ashore waiting for him up on top.

I rarely spoke up at our weekly safety meetings, but this time I put in my two bits' worth. We had been discussing things like the need to wear safety belts and keeping our work space clean, when I raised my hand. "It's all very well to talk about safety here on board, but we nearly got killed coming out here because the pilot took off in a thunderstorm."

The tool pusher gave me an icy stare. "It's up to you," he said. "You can decline to get aboard the helicopter any time you decide you don't want to."

Holly came to meet me at the heliport for the last time on June 21st. I had it in mind that we might somehow resolve our problems by talking things out. I wondered if my diminishing sexual desire was a consequence bred of familiarity, or if I was becoming fed up with her apparent inability to get her life together. Perhaps she was grandstanding because she sensed she could never hurt me the way Mary had. But all my speculating came to an end when we got to the apartment. This time it wasn't a key I found but a pair of underwear.

"What the hell is this?"

Holly looked at me with wide-eyes, feigning nonchalance. "What do you expect?"

"Well, this just about does it. I'm not going to pay the rent on this place so you can shack up while I'm gone."

"So what were you doing at Kerrville?"

"I wasn't fucking somebody's old lady in his own house, by God. And I wasn't with no low-life thieving junkie either."

It came to me in a flash that I knew the owner of the underwear. He was a sometime equipment man for Rex and Mickey. Suddenly, our apartment seemed very small. I had no plan of action, but then one came to me. It didn't take five minutes to pack. All I had was a suitcase, my guitar, and a typewriter. My other move involved a phone call to a slim, dark-eyed schoolteacher.

"Can you come get me? I'm in a bind over here."

The voice on the line sounded surprised, "Sure."

"Great, I'll explain later. I'll be outside waiting on the street."

To Holly I turned and said, "You can have this place and we'll see if your boyfriend can come up with the rent."

So it happened. I changed partners and moved into Angie's place on Q Street. I didn't even have a car by then, having traded in the perfectly good Ford my mom had given me for an International Harvester pickup that didn't get me fifty miles. One more bad decision, but I wasn't looking back. And so it happened the following week that a new woman drove me down the beach road over San Luis Pass, past the Jesus Is Lord Surf Shop and the stinking Dow Chemical plants to the heliport at Freeport.

I didn't last much longer on *Sedneth I*, quitting after a few more hitches. My record was finally coming out and we had a release party planned for August 18th at Anderson Fair. Meanwhile, offshore, we had another blowout. Not nearly so frightening as the one before, it merely blew the bushings out of the rotary-table and broke the driller's leg. It also happened during one of my weeks ashore what I got a rose tattoo, which pained my mother greatly.

"No one in our family has ever had a tattoo."

"Well, I guess you can't say that anymore."

JJ Wanker showed up on the Island and we ran amok for a couple of days. Then, inevitably, I ran into Rex. "I can't believe you stole my girlfriend."

"I didn't steal anybody."

"You stole her."

"Rex, in case you don't remember, it was you who introduced me to Angie."

"I just can't believe you would go and do a thing like that.'

"Rex, what I believe is you set us up because you didn't want to go steady."

"I didn't want to go steady, that's true, but I didn't intend for you to steal her."

"I didn't steal her, she went along with the deal."

"I can't believe it. She was one of my best girlfriends, and you stole her."

In Texas Last December

The records finally came from the pressing plant late in July. Rex and I took his van to pick them up at a truck depot over on the north side of Houston. We were both amazed at the amount of space taken up by a thousand LPs.

"Wow, you've got a record out now. You're famous."

"I don't know, man. Where are we gonna put all these things?"

I didn't feel so famous, but I felt pretty good. Vindicated maybe. I had worked a deal with a guy named Charlie Bickley of Buttermilk Records. Charlie owned the studio in the Heights where we had done the mixing, and we agreed to put the record out under his logo.

Back on the rig, I sold my first copy to one Ernie Johnson of Manny, Louisiana. I quit after one more hitch, "drug up" as they say in the oil patch. If I wasn't yet famous, maybe I was going to be. In any case, Angie had a real job. I also made arrangements to file for a divorce from Holly. I was moving on and I wasn't looking back.

The release party at Anderson Fair went well. A music scene was beginning to happen there, and a good crowd showed up. While I was by no means the first person to produce my own record, it wasn't so common then, and it was plenty of reason to celebrate. The first week of October, I flew back to Nashville where I got a Rent-a-Wreck car, an early sixties Impala, and drove out to Townes and Cindy's cabin in Williamson County. Located on eight hundred acres of woods and pasture, it was more a sharecropper's shack than a cabin. Like Seymour's old place, it had running water but no flush toilet. Townes seemed cheerful, though Cindy was moody as ever. Living with Townes would wear anybody down, I figured. He had bought her a horse, but she didn't have anybody to ride with.

"So, how's it going?"

"We're living off the land and turning into hillbillies out here."

Townes had a crazy friend named Michael who lived across the hollow. He warned me that Michael was Indian and got extremely loco on firewater. He would do just about anything for Townes. One of the games they played was where Townes would shoot an arrow off into the woods and bet him he couldn't find it. Michael would be gone half an hour then come back triumphantly with the arrow.

But I wasn't so pleased when Michael drank all my whiskey within the space of ten minutes before he stomped off. "That's some kind of friend you got there."

"He's okay. You've just gotta understand."

"I understand he drank the whole pint by himself. That's not okay."

"We can go get some more."

"That ain't the point."

"Well, if he comes back with a gun we might have to shoot him."

"You shoot him then. He's your friend."

Michael didn't come back. Townes and I drove to the liquor store in Franklin where we bought another jug. He said that Michael was really an okay guy and not to worry about him. The next day, he came by with a wounded hawk he was taking care of. Townes was right about Michael. He was okay without the firewater.

I had come back to Nashville to visit and take some copies of my record around. Among the people to whom I gave copies were John Lomax, Ed Penney, Travis Rivers, and Jack Clement. While I was there, I wrote a song called "Coyote Waltz," about the trickster "Little Brother," as the Indians called him, living in

Los Angeles. Maybe it was about Townes too. I decided to record it on my next album, already in the planning stages.

In November, I went back to Bill's camp up on the Trinity. He didn't seem any less friendly because Holly and I had split the blanket. I didn't go into any details or try to explain anything. That night I heard coyotes for real, and an owl whose cry sounded like a girl. The morning came up foggy as I stood in a two-track waiting for first light. A skunk walked right by me, never looking up. I eased slowly down the road which bordered a sorghum field. Suddenly, two deer took off running through the mist. Carelessly, I shot after them, knowing I wouldn't connect. I only wanted to smell powder burning and feel the gun buck against my shoulder.

I wrote several songs over the winter: "Walking My Blues Away," "So Long Gone," with Mickey White, and "Over All Over," a waltz I wrote for Freddy Fender. In February, I mailed out the first edition of what would become *Poor Richard's Newsletter*. Angie and I were still living in the apartment on Q Street, a sorry rat hole full of cockroaches. Quiet and sweet natured, Angie was no housekeeper. But she didn't give me any trouble, and she was manifestly not crazy. For that I was grateful.

One afternoon, I cut my hand washing dishes. It happened that an emergency crew with their ambulances were located across the street, and I walked over, holding the wound shut with my good hand. "You've got a pretty good cut there, you better go to the clinic and get that sewed up." He directed me to the clinic at the UTMB hospital, where I was attended by a lady doctor. She held my hand and I felt a tingle, a flood of warmth.

"What happened?"

"I cut myself washing dishes."

"We're going to need to close this up." It didn't take her all that long to clean and stitch up the wound. She was so intently absorbed in her work I don't think she was aware I was staring at her, almost in disbelief. It didn't hurt, and the warm tingling never stopped. I would have gladly had her doctor me all day long. Angie saw my bandaged hand when she came back from school. "What happened?"

"I cut myself and had to get a couple of stitches. They didn't even charge me."

The first review of *In Texas Last December* appeared in the *Houston Chronicle*. Dale Adamson wrote, "Dobson writes in the pithy down-to-earth style that is at the heart of country music. He traffics in down-and-outism and that spirit –whatever it may be –that gets people through hard times and toughens them without numbing their sensitivity."

Looking back, I can't say I expected sudden fame and success, but I figured the next step was to put a band together. The lineup consisted of Charlie Bickley on bass, Mike Edwards on drums, Andre Mathews on lead guitar, and Owen Cody on fiddle. Calling ourselves The Dick 'n The Dirt Band, we played a number of gigs around Houston and Galveston, including opening for David Allan Coe at the Texas Opry House. Though we didn't last as a unit, we would go on to play together again in various combinations, including an expanded electric version of the Hemmer Ridge Mountain Boys with Rex and Mickey.

But I was feeling restless again and tired of being broke. I still didn't have any wheels and needed some dental work. Besides, Rock Romano and I had begun work on another record, and I knew of no other way to raise money and pay for studio time. I was like a man building a boat in his backyard, working on a dream a little at a time to sail away. March found me back out on *Sedneth I*, drilling oil and shivering in a late season blue norther.

I signed on for twenty-one straight days, passing my thirty-sixth birthday offshore. I was too old for roughnecking, but I was hooked on the danger, the clash of iron, the sheer size and power of the draw works and the rotary-table. My birthday passed like any other day, and I don't know if I even thought about Skinny Dennis on the third anniversary of his death. One of the young roughnecks was much impressed when I told him I knew Dusty Hill of ZZ Top. Actually I knew his brother, Rocky Hill, better. Going under the alias of Heck Doolin, Rocky had played lead guitar on some of the tracks of my record.

"But it's tough," I said, "getting your foot in the door with the music business."

The young roughneck spit for emphasis. "Not if you kick hard enough."

The Reaper Collects

One afternoon, word came that we were moving to the shipyard and that *Sedneth I* was headed across the water to Nigeria. Built in Holland, the floating behemoth had already crossed the Atlantic once. Scuttlebutt had it she was getting too old to pass U.S. Coast Guard inspection. In any case, she had drilled her last well in American waters. On the morning of March 20th, we pulled the last of the retrievable casings out of the hole, then the divers went down to cap the well at the bottom. We tidied up the rig floor, chaining down anything that might move. The other crew began pulling anchors after we had gone off tour.

The next morning we floated, towering high above the water, exposing forty or fifty feet of seaweed and barnacles on the sides of the pontoons and pilings. The waiting tugboats had hooked up to the rig while we slept. We had an easy day chipping and painting and talking about our upcoming move. I wondered what the trip across the ocean might be like.

The following day came up foggy, but the sun soon burned off the haze. We were moving somewhere off the Bolivar coast. Our destination was the shipyard at Sabine. The sky cleared by mid-afternoon. The rig heaved slowly and we could hear the drone of the tugboat engines sending long black plumes of exhaust trailing away to the north.

We came out on deck the next morning to find ourselves totally enshrouded in fog with a visibility of less than fifty feet. A pale sun rose overhead. It took us all day to make a few miles up the muddy channel. The next day, Thursday the 23rd, we made it to our berth on the west bank of the Sabine River. We had already cut loose from the big offshore tugs. A smaller craft had begun working down below when we went off tour. My bag and guitar packed and ready, I was lying on my bunk wondering if Angie might already be waiting down in the parking lot. Then I heard screams and the sound of retching in the hall.

"Oh Goddamn, did you see that!"

"Man, I'm gonna puke. That makes me sick!"

"Poor son of a bitch."

Some of the off duty crew had been hanging out, smoking at the rail, watching the tug below setting one of our anchor lines. The boat had turned sideways in the current and the cable had jumped out from the posts that held it evenly astern. Springing free, the cable whipped across and cut a deckhand in half, killing him instantly. Bobby, the radio man and medic, was the first to go down. He came back up to the galley later, looking pale and drew himself a cup of coffee. The man was already dead and there was nothing to do but wait for the ambulance to come from Port Arthur and take him away.

Angie was there to meet me in the parking lot when they finally let us go about ten-thirty. Any joy I might have felt at getting off the rig after twenty-two days was overshadowed by the accident. Word had spread that the deckhand was only nineteen and had a wife and new baby. He had just come on board that afternoon. After hanging around us for months, the Reaper had finally scored.

"Did you see the ambulance?"

"Yes, I was worried about you."

"It wasn't one of us. A guy got killed down on one of the boats."

"God, that's awful. I'm glad it wasn't you."

"Yeah, he was only a kid and his wife just had a baby."

"How do you know that?"

"I don't know, it's one of the first things we heard."

We didn't talk much on the ride to Galveston. I was thinking how death could come and snatch you at any moment. There was an underwater video camera mounted down at the well head that stayed on while we were drilling. You could watch the television monitor in the drillers shack up on the floor and see the big jewfish down there with swirling streams of smaller fish whirling around. Every once in a while, merely by opening its mouth, the little fish were sucked in, while all around, the swirling dance went on. Death was like that. I was beginning to notice how living constantly was this notion in my head was changing the way I looked at life.

A week later, I was back on board. The rig was a mess, swarming with welders and other contracted help. Sleeping was impossible with the sounds of hammering and voices in the hall by the starboard anchor winch, watching my thin trickle arch its way down to join the muddy river blow. The words of the "Texas River Song" came to mind, a traditional tune I had first heard from Houston folksinger Don Sanders. Townes had given me the lyrics back in Nashville in October.

> *The girls of the river they're plump and they're pretty*
> *The Sabine and Sulphur got beauties plenty*
> *On the banks of the Nechez, there's girls by the score*
> *But I never will roll by the Brazos no more.*

Another twelve hours of drudgery. Another day in the life gone behind me. I smoked a joint out on the rail after dinner, watching the lights, the tugs, working boats, and tankers headed upstream to the refineries of Beaumont and Port Arthur, thinking of the deckhand who had got himself killed on the hitch before. I wondered if it was just a special kind of love that made him go to the boats. If it were just another job and nothing more, he would have been better off stocking groceries or selling shoes, and maybe he would still be alive to come home each evening to his wife and baby. But you never knew. You could be killed just as easily in a car wreck when your number came up.

Back in the room, I played guitar. I was interrupted by my roommates' grinning entry with two smuggled six-packs of beer. As I later wrote in my newsletter, you didn't tell a pair of nineteen-year old Mississippi roughnecks they couldn't have a beer after work. Not with the wine shop located just up the road. Clearly, there were advantages to working in the shipyard. Still, I wished I were back up in Houston where the Hemmer Ridge Mountains Boys were playing that weekend with the legendary bluesman Lightning Hopkins.

The Shipyard

I hated shipyard work. The last time I had done it was on the D.J. Bokencamp, a three-legged jack-up rig I worked on in Jacintoport, the town so-named after the battleground nearby, where Sam Houston and the Texicans had routed Santa Anna some 130 years before. I followed that rig to Long Island in the Bahamas, where I pulled two twenty-day hitches and they worked us like dogs as much as sixteen hours a day. There were no blacks working offshore then, let alone women, and you could be fired if your hair was too long.

But the work itself was unchanging. We spent half a day cleaning parts in the motor room and after lunch set to work chipping on the starboard anchor winch, the one that nearly gobbled me up the year before. I shivered at the memory. Later that evening, I was talking to a girl in the galley who asked me about the record. "Yeah, I put it out myself."

"So you play music professionally?

"Well, not professional enough, or I wouldn't be here."

It rankled, but I had a plan. The old *Sedneth I* was going to take me to Europe and I was going to be paid for an ocean voyage in the process. In the meantime, there was one good thing about the shipyard: you could go down after work and put your feet down on solid ground in the evening. You could ride down and drink a few beers in the parking lot and listen to Fleetwood Mac and Lynyrd Skynyrd and Jimmie Buffet on the tape deck while looking up at the rig towering above us like a great ocean liner.

Our elevator consisted of a winch line shackled to a cargo basket. On a Wednesday, the hitch over, I signaled for the roustabout to take me up to pick up my gear. I was back on the deck when he hit me with some bad news. "The tool pusher says we gotta work over or be fired."

"Bullshit. I finished my hitch. I'm going to the house." I was feeling my beers.

The roustabout shrugged, "Don't blame me. I'm just passing on what I heard."

Trouble beckoned when I decided to go back ashore for a couple of hours to think things over. My companions were Marvin, a motorman from Mississippi, Connie, who had dropped out of UT law school, and Mike, a derrick man. The four of us drove to Port Arthur, where we drank two-fifths of whiskey in a rough looking brown bag joint with Spanish songs on the jukebox. Mike was black, but nobody gave us any trouble about it. Port Arthur was Janis Joplin's home town. I told the guys I had once poured tequila for her and some friends when I was tending bar in New York in the fall of 1969. Nearly ten years had gone by. Plenty drunk, the four of us stumbled back to the rig where I stayed just long enough to grab my bag and guitar.

I caught a ride with one of the first cars that went by, a refinery worker who was headed down the coast road to Galveston. What he hit me with, and why, remains a mystery. Maybe he got mad after I passed out in his truck. I was bleeding when I came to out on the road at the ferry landing on the Galveston side. At least he threw my bag and guitar out of his truck before taking off. Bleeding, I cried after him as the taillights sped away, "You dirty son of a bitch. You hit me."

A lady cop gave me a ride to the emergency room where I was given some stitches, and I called Angie to come get me. Blood-soaked, I knew I had a minor concussion, but I was lucky. I could have been killed and dumped along the lonely coast road. A couple of days later, the office called to verify where my plane ticket was to be sent, so I hadn't been fired after all. The first leg of the ninety day tow to Nigeria would be from the mouth of the Sabine to Barbados. I would take the second part from there across the Atlantic to the Cape Verde Islands. Not only was I not fired, but I had a month off with pay to work on the new record. I was embarking on a new adventure. All the miseries of the past weeks were behind, if not forgotten, and life looked good.

A Regrettable Episode

Angie, JJ Wanker, and I were headed out of the Southwest Freeway in Houston when we saw that Emmylou Harris was playing that evening at the Summit, the hall for Rockets basketball and for big music shows. JJ and I were on a tear, which may have accounted for my lack of judgment and an unfortunate notion which overtook me.

"Hey guys, let's go say hello to Rodney Crowell. He's playing with Emmylou tonight."

"How do you know where to find him?"

"That's easy, they'll be staying next door at the Stouffer Hotel. That's were Willie stays when he plays the Summit. I was there last year."

"Hmm, so what makes you think Rodney will be there?"

"Well, it's worth a shot. Angie, do you want to meet Rodney?"

"Sure."

"Maybe we can get some complimentary tickets," I said, warming to the idea.

I was right about being able to find Rodney, but way wrong in figuring he would be happy to see us. We had been friends and roommates back in the early days, and I was learning that those were the days that were no more. Of course, I had no way of knowing his parents were going to be there when I rang him up from the lobby.

"Hey Rodney, how's it going?"

"Where are you calling from?"

"We're right down here in the lobby."

Paranoia suggested itself, a creeping realization that came with the pause at the other end. "Well, come on up."

Rodney met us at the door. "How did you know where to find me?"

"It was easy, I asked for your name at the desk." I explained about Willie. Rodney ushered us in and introduced me to his parents. I introduced Angie and JJ, and we shook hands all around. When I got a closer look at him, I could see Rodney looked wide-eyed and stressed, perhaps a bit wired. At the same time, I was conscious of feeling a little uncool, like there was some *faux pas* or *gaffe*, little French words for a fuckup, in the making. Settling back in a chair, Rodney's dad seemed friendly and noncommittal. As for Rodney's mom, I wasn't sure if she recognized me as the one who had married Rodney's old girlfriend, but I was reasonably sure she didn't like what she saw. Still, I attempted to engage her in some small talk.

"I guess you must be very proud of your son for doing so well these days."

"Why, yes, we are, and we're very proud of our daughter-in-law too."

"Yes, of course. I'm sure you are." Touché. I had forgotten that Rodney had recently married Rosanne Cash, daughter of the Man in Black. Rodney was not merely doing well, he had married into country music aristocracy. The room seemed crowded. I noticed that JJ had gone back out into the hall.

Rodney was moving towards the door. "I've got to go to sound check now."

"Mind if we tag along?" I was curious to see how they set up sound in a big place like the Summit.

"No man, I really don't think that would be cool." Rodney's eyes were cold blue. "Maybe I can get you some tickets for the show tonight."

I failed to understand what was so important about a sound check, but it was plainly time to leave and we did. We made our goodbyes, and I told Rodney we would wait to hear from him in the bar downstairs. It was then, overcome by shame and remorse, I began fighting back the tears. JJ was waiting by the elevator.

"Hey, while you were talking with Rodney's folks, I was talking with Emmylou in the hall. She's real nice."

"Sure man, let's go have a drink."

The elevator door opened, and we rode down. I was crushed and couldn't hold back the tears anymore. Rodney and I had been friends, but the times had changed. Years later, I ran into his cousin who had been there and said, in fact, he had come looking for us with tickets for the show. We had waited in the bar, but I guess we left before he got there. Back on the Island and still feeling stung, I mailed him a copy of my new album. "Dear Rodney," I wrote, "Kiss my ass."

The Rabbit

Angie and I had settled into a routine. Her housekeeping was deplorable, but we had good sex and I enjoyed her soft spoken nature. She was almost apologetic when she said she was late with her period.
  "I'm a month late and I think I might be pregnant."
  "What about the pill?"
  "I must have missed a day."
  "How could you do that?"
  "I'm not sure."
  "Well, don't worry about it. Let's go get a test kit. At least that way we'll know."
  Half disbelieving, I drove to the drug store for a test kit. I've forgotten how it worked but there was something about a rabbit. The rabbit was supposed to die. Or the rabbit didn't die. The rabbit was teaching me to tie a bowline, a handy knot for making a loop that neither slips nor jams. The rabbit went into the hole, around the tree, and back into the hole again. Then he died. Or maybe they didn't use rabbits anymore, but we had been doing it like bunnies. Now Angie was pregnant. Happy Easter.
  The next day, we drove up to Houston and dropped by my parents' house. They were not home, so I left a note taped to the refrigerator door. "Dear Folks, we have news of more than passing interest." I didn't know what to think about the news. The discovery had an air of inevitability about it, of finality, a done deal that I had never been consulted about. Of course, having

broken the news—however obliquely—to my parents ruled out the possibility of an abortion. Not that I was sure I wanted one. Lots of people I knew had kids and it didn't seem to mean the end of the world for them.

Angie and I were married by a judge in Galveston sometime during the month before I rejoined *Sedneth I* in Barbados. I recalled a theological distinction, unctuously intoned by a black-cassocked celibate whose vows forbade him to marry, that *to marry* is an active verb. You did not get married as we commonly say; you marry someone. For reasons of her own, my mother chose not to count my marriage to Holly, from whom I had been divorced only a few weeks. But I counted this as my fourth official wedding. If I had the feeling my life was slipping out of control, there was no course but to go on and make the best of it. Angie would join me in London after the rig tow, so she would get a European honeymoon out of the deal. Or maybe, I thought, the rig might capsize and she would collect the insurance money.

Outward Bound

On a Sunday, I flew out of Houston Intercontinental to Miami, where the crew assembled were easily recognizable in their boots and Levis, Western shirts, and redneck tans. The company had arranged for us to stay overnight at a hotel near the airport. After dinner, Matt, Red, and I decided to go bowling. Already thinking of England, I chose Winston for my bowling name. We ended up at a disco later, where we encountered some hostile stares from the locals as we stomped around oafishly. Never mind. They took our money and nobody messed with us. We had a lot of drinks. I vaguely remembered trying to hustle some woman, but I woke up alone, good and hung over, the next morning.

After some delays at the airport, we boarded a charter flight: a prop-plane to take us to Barbados with a stop in San Juan, Puerto Rico. We were supposed to fly on, but the plane needed something repaired so we had an extra night ashore where some of us went sight-seeing in the old colonial party of the city.

"Barbados, Barbados, oh what a beautiful island—" These words from a Jesse Colin Young song drifted through my mind as we descended, banked, and landed. Easternmost of the Windward Islands, only 166 square miles with nothing but an ocean ahead of us all the way to Africa. We taxied to a halt and deplaned, milling like cattle through a big customs shed. I hadn't anticipated any trouble. It was just as well nobody poked through my bag, which contained a stash of pot rolled up in a pair of socks. A bus took us to our hotel, which was situated some distance from the town.

Dropping my bag off in the room, I set out to investigate. It was early afternoon, with no one around at the hotel bar. I walked out to the street to get my bearings where I was approached by a kid on a bike.

"You from a ship, mon?"

"Not exactly, it's a drilling rig. Do you know what that is?"

"No, mon."

"Well, it's like a ship, it floats. Tell me, where's the action around here? I don't see any bars."

"They're all downtown, mon"

"Where's the liquor store?"

"What you like, mon? I can get it for you."

"How about a bottle of rum, they make good rum here, don't they?"

"Oh yeah, mon, the best. You want marijuana? I can get you some."

"No, but I would like a bottle of rum."

I gave the kid some money and watched him disappear on his bicycle. After a while Matt, one of my roommates came out.

"What's happening?"

"Waiting on a bottle of rum."

"All right."

"At least I hope I am." It occurred to me I might have made a mistake trusting the kid with the money, but he returned directly, carrying my bottle in a paper sack. He grinned as I opened it to look inside. The label had a picture of two fighting rosters and was called Cockspur Rum.

"Hey Matt, this kid here says he can get you some pot. He just brought this jug for me." I looked the bottle over. I had been expecting Mount Gay. "Is this good rum?"

"It's the very best, mon. Make your dick hard—you fuck all night long."

But the kid was wrong, not that it wasn't good rum. The better part of it, added to whatever we were drinking at the whorehouse in Bridgeport where Matt, Red, and I went for our last fling ashore, had rather the opposite effect. What can you do with a drunken sailor? When the moment of truth finally came to test his claim, I had rendered myself impotent, though by then I scarcely cared.

We got only an hour's sleep before they rousted us out in the morning and bused us to the harbor where we ferried out to the rig. *Sedneth I* stood a couple of miles offshore, tied close to the *Oceana*, out of Bremen, an ocean-going tug the size of small ship. The departing crew looked mighty glad to see us, but there was no time for visiting as we put our traveling clothes away, pulled on our steel-toed boots, and donned our hard hats. Rocking in the Atlantic swells, we left Barbados behind as the *Oceana* payed out the towing line until it stood out nearly a mile in front of us.

The tool pusher put me and Matt to work making up a high pressure piece of blowout-preventer equipment, an enormous hunk of steel. The bolts had to be tightened with an impact wrench and a sledgehammer. Matt held the wrench, tied to a piece of line, while I hammered. It was better to use the line as a safety precaution, since a misplaced blow from the hammer could turn a finger to mush. As we tightened one nut, the others loosened imperceptibility. We kept working our way around clockwise in a circle. I had a fierce headache, pounding in unison with the hammer.

Matt offered to help. "Here, let me spell you off."

"No, man I got it."

I worked furiously, concentrating on my work. The perfectly swung hammer blow was like a pool shot slamming into the picket, Zen-perfect, while a missed blow risked dangerous and unpredictable results. After a while, I let Matt spell me off while I held the wrench for him.

Later that afternoon, as Barbados slowly dropped astern we were seated on a narrow I-beam, working high above the steel deck. I needed a tool on the other side where we were working. I could have stayed put and scooted myself along to retrieve it. Might have, could have, should have, but I walked the beam with cold, hung-over lucidity. I never looked down and the deck did not rush up to meet me. I wasn't going to fall. I had gone beyond all my should-haves and ought-tos. I should have been back in Nashville writing songs instead of riding a drilling rig across the ocean. Driven by my thirst for adventure, my relentless pursuit of the ineffable, I was taking it one more step, looking for the mystical connection, living on the edge for a glimpse, a taste of the beyond.

Grass Fires

We had easy work on the thirty-two day crossing. With no drilling to be done, everyone worked maintenance, with all but the watch standers on the day shift. We were surrounded by a vast expanse of water, a fact that never left my consciousness, day or night. After a couple of days, we saw no birds, no fish, no ships, nor planes. The first few nights I was frequently awakened by the big Atlantic swells booming against the pontoons. Moving at an average speed of 2.5 knots, we made about sixty to seventy miles a day. Riding awkwardly under tow, *Sedneth I* pitched and rolled in a corkscrew motion I never got used to.

My companions were Matt and Red, young roughnecks from Balinger, Texas. Both were into pot and rock 'n roll. There was Ray, the driller and our immediate boss, who was not. There was Hank the welder, a Vietnam veteran. There was Herb the tool pusher, and Bobby the medic and radio-man. It was Bobby who had gone down to try and help the deckhand who had been killed back at the shipyard in Sabine. We were 130 miles out of Barbados when he poked his nose into our room; we were sitting around shooting the breeze after dinner.

"What's going on?" He gave us a funny look.

"Not much, come on in."

"No, I can't right now." Bobby turned, closing the door behind him.

"What's with him?" Matt asked.

"I don't know, dumb pecker head." Red didn't like Bobby much.

A few minutes later there came a knock on the door. It was Bobby with Herb, who came straight to the point. "Bobby tells me he smelled marijuana in your room."

"No sir, no way." Red was indignant.

"You must be smelling my grass rug." Matt smiled. "We ain't been smoking nothing. I bought that rug back in Puerto Rico."

"You guys ain't been smoking nothing?" Herb walked over and sniffed at the rug which was rolled up on an upper bunk.

"No sir."

Bobby tried to rescue himself. "I swear I smelled smoke in here."

"If I catch anybody using drugs or marijuana on this rig I'm going to have them prosecuted, is that understood?"

"Yes sir."

Herb and Bobby walked out, closing the door behind them. We waited a few seconds before erupting in a gleeful round of high-fives.

"Hey Matt, what do you say let's roll up some of that rug and try it out."

"I don't know, we better be careful."

Red was still angry. "What an idiot! I'd like to kick his ass, that little son of a bitch."

"I'll tell you what, boys. I wouldn't worry about it," I said. "I don't believe he's going to be bothering us anymore this trip. I believe he's done shot his wad."

Crossing Over

My prediction about Bobby was right. He had blown his credibility and never bothered us again. Word got out, even among the hands who didn't smoke, that he had made a fool of himself. Despised as a brown nose and a squealer, he had already gotten somebody fired on the other crew. But our contempt turned to pity somewhere in mid-ocean where word came over the radio that his boy had been killed back home in a car wreck. Death had brushed him twice that summer, and all the cockiness went out of him.

There wasn't much exercise in chipping and painting all day. In the evenings, I took to running laps up on the helicopter deck with the sun in decline over the vast, empty sea. Later, we gathered by the starboard anchor winch, still the best spot where we could enjoy a smoke unobserved with a clear view of anybody coming. Everyone was getting laid off after the two anyway, so the threat of firing carried little weight. As for the threat of prosecution, Herb was leaning on a slender reed and he must have known it, because he never bothered us again, either.

In the evenings, there were movies in the recreation room, though they didn't bring enough to last the trip. After a couple of weeks, there was nothing to watch but reruns, but the men didn't seem to mind. On Sundays we had the day off, something unheard of when we were drilling, and barbecued steaks up on the helicopter deck. One afternoon, I sat in the galley listening to Hank, the welder, tell war stories. Hank was quiet, and I had never talked much with him before. He said he had spent three years as an advisor to the South Vietnamese army, back in the days before the major buildup of U.S. troops began. It seemed like a lot of the older hands had been in the war, including most of the helicopter pilots.

"What about the My Lai Massacre?" I asked.

"Calley got framed, man. That shit happened all the time. All the time. Wasting villages was just routine."

The days went by slowly as the sun rode across the sky. Armies of cumulus clouds marched from horizon to horizon, banked against blazing fire as the blue ocean turned back and the stars came out wheeling in the night sky. The days grew warmer as we crawled toward the equator, toward Africa, making 2.6 to 2.8 knots on a course of 84 degrees. Every night I visited the barge control room to record our position at 1800 hours and watch the level bubbles, one for pitch and one for roll.

Eleven days out, I spotted the only ship I was to see the whole crossing. She was hull down and lonesome on the horizon, heading north-west. I had finished a book on coyotes I had brought with me written by the Texas historian J. Frank Dobie, and had started on *Voyage* by Sterling Hayden, a sea novel of square-rigger days sailing round Cape Horn. On June 9th, our position report read latitude 15 degrees 36 minutes by longitude 42 degrees 53 minutes. Still heading at 84 degrees, we had come 1016 miles with 1009 remaining to Cape Verde. We had reached the halfway point and were on the downhill side.

June 11th, a Sunday, came up cool and overcast with a fresh breeze. I tried to call Angie but couldn't raise the overseas operator. Most of the men had already called their wives, but after trying once, I didn't bother again. Down below us, the seas crashed against the pontoons, shooting up spray from the cresting waves as we plowed ahead.

On June 13th, Red and I were assigned to chipping and painting the mud room where, during normal operations, the drilling fluid is circulated, tested, and mixed. It was hot and noisy inside with the needle guns clattering against the steel walls, and we took frequent breaks to lean on the rail and stare out over the water. The mud tanks themselves were stacked full of cases of canned goods, far more than we would consume on the tow, stored for future use. It was in there, bored and rummaging around, that I spied a case of Big Chief Vanilla Extract.

"Hey Red, look here what I found."

"What you got, man?"

"It says here this stuff is thirty-five percent alcohol. That's seventy proof."

"Did you try it?"

"Not yet." I twisted off the cap of one of the bottles and gingerly took a sip. "Man, this stuff will get you high, I guarantee it."

"No shit. Lemme try some." Red scrunched up his face and passed the bottle back. We had a couple slugs apiece and went back to work. Results were not long in coming, though it was not an altogether pleasant buzz, owing perhaps to the powerful aftertaste of vanilla. Still, it broke the monotony, and I brought a bottle back to the room to see if it would mix into a more palatable cocktail. We had a Big Chief party that night, mixing drinks with pineapple juice. I awoke the next morning with a headache. I didn't know about Matt and Red. That afternoon I saw a land bird, some kind of martin or swallow, a long way from any land. While chipping paint on the stairs leading up to the helicopter deck, I could see the twin flags of the Netherlands and the United States whipping in the breeze, with Old Glory frayed back nearly to the stars. From somewhere there came the sizzle of welding.

In the final days, we continued to gather and smoke by the starboard anchor winch, scarcely attempting to hide anymore. I played guitar in the evenings. Matt and Red enjoyed listening, but I didn't know any of the rock songs they asked me to play. Increasingly, they began to talk about what they were going to do when they got back home to Balinger. I found another book, *Snowblind*, about cocaine smuggling back when it was done by amateurs. Trimming my new beard, I looked in the mirror and tried to imagine the prospect of family life as far below us the waves slammed into the pontoons and we shuddered on towards Cape Verde. On the night of June 20th, I could see a full moon from our window, moving in a slow arc as we pitched and rolled. It drifted behind some clouds for a moment, then broke free in an explosion of silver radiance.

In the daylight, the old *Sedneth I* shone like new with every square foot of deck, bulkhead, and machinery freshly painted. Work was slowing down and the men tended to gather at the rail to talk and gaze at the horizon. I began a series of daydreams of old girlfriends, going back to my first love when I was in college; of a girl down in Cali, after I had dropped out and first wandered; of my first wife Nanci in Michigan and Chile; of a girl in New Mexico; of Mary in Tennessee; of Holly; and now, I thought of Angie. I thought about all the rambling between and wondered if I was finally ready to settle down. I was not at all sure I ever would. It seemed like all my friends in the music world lived for the moment without much thought of slowing, much less settling, down. "Where you've been is good and gone, all you keep is the getting there," wrote Townes. And that didn't leave room for much else.

On June 23rd, heading on a course now of eighty degrees, we had come 1,978 miles, the same number as the year. The next morning around nine o'clock, we raised the barren headlands of the outermost of the Cape Verde Islands. Emerging from a bank of clouds, they reminded me of the Sandia Mountains outside Albuquerque. All day we watched from the port side, where we could see the cliffs and lava flows, a moonscape with great white plumes of spray where the waves hit the rocks. That evening I copied our position report for the last time. Latitude 16 degrees, 52 minutes N by 25 degrees 13 minutes W, heading 75 degrees. Wind E, 16 knots. Swell NE, 3-5 feet. Speed, 2.8 knots. Cape Verde, thirteen miles.

Country Matters

Red, Matt, Connie, and I were all a little drunk when we rode down the personnel net for the last time, waving good-bye to old *Sedneth I* where we had put in so much sweat and toil and had enjoyed some good times in spite of it all. In the confusion and excitement before we left, Connie had traded five gallons of red lead-primer for a bottle of Jim Beam whiskey, a deal executed in broad daylight with a man down below us in a pitching rowboat. The bucket went down on a line and the bottle came back up. For all of our nightly pot smoking and pilfering of Big Chief, I was amazed at this brazen act.

Cape Verde looked desolate and forlorn, like a place the world had forgotten. Once through Customs, a bus took us to the airport. We boarded a charter flight to Dakar on the African coast, where we waited several hours for an Air France overnight flight to Paris. The next morning, I said good-bye to Matt and Red. We had become good friends on the trip and I had tried to talk them into hanging out for a few days. Red wavered, but in the end they both only wanted to get back home to Balinger, Texas.

"Are you sure you don't want to take some time and hang around?"

"No, man, I'm going to the house."

"Well so long, boys. We'll see you down the road." We shook hands and that was the last I ever saw of them, standing with the rest of the crew in their Western shirts and cowboy boots, looking even stranger and out of place than they had looked back in Miami.

Of the whole crew, only one person elected to stay and take advantage of a free ride to Europe; a roustabout named Pete who had a friend we could crash with for a couple of days in Bath, England. We took the underground into Paris where we made our way to the Gare de Nord and bought tickets for London. Arriving at Victoria Station in late afternoon, we switched trains and made it to his friend's flat shortly after dark. Pete and I had a good time walking around Bath and drinking in the pubs. I found I still had my sea legs and could stare out a window and feel the horizon move. On June 28th, I said good-bye and took an early train back to London Victoria where I caught a train to Gatwick airport. Angie's plane was due to arrive at nine o'clock.

I had no trouble picking her out from among the arriving passengers. Wearing a full length yellow coat I recognized as having belonged to my mother—the sort of coat an older lady might wear—Angie looked stressed and exhausted, and I felt sorry for her. A third-generation BOI, she was the only one in her family to graduate from college. It struck me as a possibility that she had never flown before. Some wine didn't travel well, I figured, but I resolved to put a lid on it and make the best of things. I waved and came forward to help her carry her stuff.

"Hi, how was your flight?"

"It was okay. I'm glad to see you."

"It's nice to see you, too."

Back in London, we found an acceptable hotel where we stayed two nights and did tourist things, taking in the West End, Soho, Big Ben, Parliament, the changing of the guard. We planned to travel up to Scotland, but first decided to visit my old college friend Mayo who was living in the country, near Banbury. We took a train on the evening of July 1st after spending an agreeable lunch and afternoon with Peter O'Brien, an avid music fan who edited and published a magazine called *Omaha Rainbow*.

Mayo Thompson had started one of the first art-rock bands in Texas, back during the so-called psychedelic era, when I was still in the Peace Corps down in Chile. They called themselves the Red

Crayola, later spelled with a 'K' after a lawsuit was threatened by the copyright owners. They had put out two albums, and later, Mayo released one on his own. He was witty and charming when he wanted to be, but I never much understood Mayo's music, which seemed to be calculated to mystify. Still, we went back a long way, and I was looking forward to seeing him again. He was putting a new band together and had a gig that night in Banbury.

Angie and I took a train to Oxford and another to Banbury, where we took a taxi to the village of Sibford Ferris. We had no trouble finding the street and house, but had to wait a couple of hours since Mayo had already gone to his gig. We sat on the curb by his front door, a cottage with a thatched roof. I was amused to find my avant garde friend living in such quaint circumstances. After a while, I noticed Angie fidgeting, as if in some discomfort.

"What's the matter?"

"I really have to use the bathroom."

"Why don't you go squat in the bushes?"

"It's more serious than that."

"Why didn't you go back at the hotel?"

"I don't know. I haven't been able to go yet."

"You mean since you've been here?" I counted back the days in my mind. "Well, you'll just have to wait a little longer."

"I don't know if I can."

Her voice sounded tiny and desperate. My mind went back to Chile with my first wife, where we had no running water and would not even have an outhouse until we dug a hole and built one. There was a corn field out in back of our shack, behind an irrigation ditch. I had found a place to squat back there and was about finished with my business when I saw a campesino kid drop his pants and dump a steaming load by the path. I was farther back among the corn rows, and he never saw me as he hitched up his pants and walked on. Not ten seconds later, a skinny dog came along and gobbled down what the kid had left there. I was learning about the campo where shit happens and dogs fend for themselves.

"Well, we're in the country here. Why don't you just walk down the road and find a spot in the bushes." It occurred to me that the country everywhere must be pretty much alike. After a few minutes, Angie came back, and I attempted to make light of things.

"Everything come out okay?"

"That's not funny."

"Well, you should have gone back at the hotel. You had plenty of chances."

Some time passed before Mayo and his wife, Christine, arrived home from his gig. I had met her years before in New York: a tall woman, thin with strawberry-blonde hair. Mayo looked dapper and I noticed he had picked up a bit of an accent. We had a cup of tea and visited a while, after which, Christine fixed us a pallet on the floor.

The next morning, Mayo and I walked down to the neighborhood store about a block away where we bought fresh bread, bacon, and eggs for breakfast. In the daylight, I could see Sibford Ferris was a village of small homes and cottages, with a pub, fields of rolling green, with everything tidy and well ordered. It wasn't really country the way I thought of it, but for that matter neither was the country in Tennessee, or anyplace else anymore.

That afternoon, I played Mayo a cassette of some rough mixes from the new record. I knew he wasn't much into country music, and that he regarded me as something of a primitive. Still, I wasn't prepared for his reaction. "Man, it sounds like your drummer is asleep."

"Yeah, I see what you mean," I said lamely.

Mayo had a rehearsal the next afternoon. That was my introduction to the punk ethos. Mayo's drummer was a young guy from New York named Jesse who played fast and hard, though, as I mentioned before, I couldn't tell what the songs were about. Later, he played me some records by the Sex Pistols and Pere Ubu, an experimental band from Ohio he was into at the time.

That night, we went to the local pub which was called Bishop's Blaize. We had a few pints, and Mayo introduced me to the owners as a visiting songwriter from the States. To my surprise, they asked if I wanted to play, and arranged a gig for me for Friday night. I was immensely pleased and excited about playing my first show in England.

We caught a ride into Banbury the next morning, where we had fliers printed that Mayo had drawn, announcing the gig. It said TEXAS RECORDING ARTIST and I thought, "Yes, that has a good ring to it." He had also drawn us a map of the town, so we had no trouble getting around. Bill-posting was easy, with plenty of available spaces for announcements of one kind or another. We spent some time wandering around window shopping and took a bus back to the village in the late afternoon. Toward the evening, Mayo proposed a walk, and we all went out on a looping tour of footpaths he explained were ancient and protected by law, even though they might pass through private land. Mayo and I walked ahead. I've forgotten the context, but I remember clearly one thing he said, "This is a great time to be alive, you know. We are going to live to see the Millennium."

"Wow. I never thought of that. Yeah, maybe so. Maybe we got a chance." I wondered what life might bring in the meantime.

On the way back, close to the house, close by the road and not in the bushes at all, lay a large turd, a BOI from across the Great Water, mute and accusing. Nothing was said, but I wondered keenly who might have noticed it and might, perhaps, have wondered how it had come to be there.

Scotland

My excitement grew as the night of my gig approached. Mayo got a PA together for me, with a big Marshall amp to play through. I made a set list, and warmed up back at the cottage. I was determined to play well and not disappoint Mayo and his New Wave friends. I could feel synchronicity at work. The place we had played back in Nashville was called Bishops, and in fact had been modeled after an English pub.

A good crowd had showed up by the time I started. I was surprised to see a number of bikers in the crowd looking very much like their American counterparts, except they didn't all ride Harleys, nor did they seem so menacing. I played two sets, finishing as the crowd surged toward the bar for last call. I received a number of compliments and a number of drinks, and even got paid a little in the bargain. After all this, we were back at the cottage by eleven.

"You sounded really good," Mayo said. "I like your new songs."

"Thanks, I appreciate that. I had a great time."

"The audience enjoyed it, too. I talked with several people who said they liked it very much."

"Thank you for making it all possible."

These remarks from Mayo and Christine filled me with a sense of well-being. Angie also seemed happy. "You played very well," she said.

Still basking in the glow of the last night's successful show, and remembering that the house guests, like fish, tend to go bad after a while, decided the next morning would be an excellent time to be moving on. Angie and I made our goodbyes and we took a cab to the station in Banbury, where we caught a train to Glasgow. We passed through some pretty country once we got past the industrial midlands. In Glasgow, we found a downtown bed and breakfast, and after dropping off our things, went out for a walk and some Chinese food. At a shop where I bought a pint of scotch, Angie, who had been too timid to speak to anyone, broke out laughing at the shopkeeper's accent. "I can't understand a word you're saying," she said. He laughed and said something back to her in a brogue so thick I didn't catch it either.

Walking back to our room, I was happy that Angie was loosening up and beginning to enjoy herself. Later, making love, I heard bells in the distance, footfalls on the sidewalk two floors below, the sounds of traffic. Glasgow was quiet, compared to London.

The next day, July 8th, we rocked on through Scotland, heading north to Inverness. From the window, I observed rabbits, wood pigeons, and curlews against a backdrop of rippling fields. We passed several rivers with good looking water, and I felt a tremendous urge to be fishing. Arriving at Inverness, we found all of the bed and breakfast places were full, but we found a nice one a ten minute walk from town: a small white house with a beautiful rose garden.

The next day, we boarded a tourist bus for Loch Ness, about an hour away. It was there we met Frank Searle, a Cockney ex-paratrooper who ran an information center and kept a camera with a telephoto lens trained on the water in case Nessie, the Loch Ness monster, might appear. He had been keeping a nine-year vigil by the lake and had made more sightings and had taken more photos than anyone. Frank sported a number of tattoos and had a better tan than one would expect for someone living in such a cold climate. His comely Belgian assistant shared his trailer and—he said with a wink—helped him with a growing volume of world-wide correspondence.

Something told me I had found my man. "How's the fishing around here?"

"Excellent. The air turns blue around my boat whenever I lose a salmon."

"Can we get a license for a day and rent equipment?" I turned to Angie. "Do you want to go fishing?"

"Sure."

"I can get you a boat and everything you need." Frank had a twinkle in his eye that reminded me of Daddy Bill back on the Trinity River. In fact, the resemblance was uncanny. I knew Bill would not have missed a chance to troll for salmon on Loch Ness. Frank made a phone call to a nearby bed and breakfast and we let the tourist bus go back to Inverness without us. He told us that he had lived for a couple of years camping out on a nearby estate owned by Led Zeppelin's Jimmy Page, and that the Inverness County Council had tried, without success, to kick him out. We also learned that the last sighting of Nessie had been on June 9th, less than a month before.

We arose early for breakfast the next morning and walked down to the Loch where Frank had a boat ready for us, along with an antique-looking trolling rod with some kind of spinner lure. "Just troll parallel to the shoreline," he said.

"All right. Thanks. Angie, you stay up in the bow. And keep your camera ready in case we see Nessie."

Frank waved as we pulled away. It was a foggy morning, and the water, stained with peat, was impenetrable. Once away from the dock, I began paying out line, feeling the throbbing pull of the spinner blades as they took hold. I remembered trolling for rainbow trout on Eagle Nest Lake in New Mexico with my father and grandfather when I was very young. Two things I remembered about my granddad were his scratchy whiskers and the pint of whiskey he always had on him. We had trolled night crawlers at the end of a yard-long series of spinners and caught our limit of big, sleek rainbow trout. My grandfather, Jim Maloney, passed on in the summer of 1958. He never got back to Ireland.

Angie and I trolled for a couple of hours, keeping close to the shoreline, which dropped steeply away. She took some pictures, but we never got a glimpse of Nessie, nor, to my disappointment, did I ever get a bite on my spinner lure. Maybe I needed a night crawler trailing behind. Frank was waiting when we returned to the dock. "Any luck?"

"No, we never even got a bite. This is a beautiful place though, I wish we had more time to hang out."

"You'll have to come back and try again."

"We will." We said goodbye to Frank and walked back to our bed and breakfast where we had made arrangements to stay over another night, there being no particular hurry for us to go. Our morning on the water had sharpened our appetites, so we set off on foot to a pub about a kilometer away. We were disappointed to find no food was being served, but we sat down and drank a couple of pints. Some of the locals, a dour, unfriendly lot, were muttering imprecations directed at a table of young German tourists. Angie began making bird noises like a ventriloquist, so no one could tell where they were coming from. I nearly fell out of my chair laughing, causing the locals to direct some unfriendly stares towards us as well. Later, we walked back and climbed the hill behind our bed and breakfast, where we found a country store and bought picnic supplies to take back to the room.

Angie and I left the next morning, catching the first bus back to Inverness, where we caught a train back the way we had come. On the afternoon of the 12th, we were back in Sibford Ferris, where we found Mayo in great form, fairly bursting with happiness on account of having passed his English driving test. "So, what's the big deal?" I asked.

"Oh, it's a very difficult test over here."

"Well, congratulations."

"Thanks. We're off to London now. You'll be all right here?"

"You bet. Thank you."

After they were gone, I browsed through Mayo's record collection. I put one on the turntable called *Animal Justice* by John Cale and turned it up a ways. It didn't take long before I heard screams coming from the other room. "Turn that down, please! I can't stand it."

"Okay baby." I took the album off the turntable and returned it to its jacket. Mayo told me later I had been playing it at the wrong speed. I assumed all twelve-inch discs played at 33 RPMs, but I had been wrong. They had twelve-inch 45s in England. Not that Angie would have liked it any better. The truth be known, I didn't like it much myself. I had put it on only to get a rise out of her.

Homeward Bound

We said good-bye to Mayo and Christine for the last time and took the train down to London, where we stayed the last couple of nights with Peter O'Brien at his flat in Surrey. With a pub down on the corner, a small grocery, and a fish & chips place, there didn't seem to be a need for more sightseeing, particularly as we were running short of money. We spent our time visiting and listening to records from Peter's huge collection. I was grateful for a place to hole up.

I put Angie on the plane at Gatwick on July 19th and took the train back to Victoria Station. I didn't realize I could have taken a shuttle bus directly to Heathrow, where my plane was due to leave the next morning. I found the airport to be noisy and crowded, with a great many American college students going home from their holidays abroad. I sat with a can of John Courage Strong Pale Ale, listening to a conversation at a table next to me. "I'm a teacher," I heard a girl say. I did not get what her companion said. A young man was playing guitar down in the Pan Am standby line, singing his heart out. I slouched down in my seat and tried to sleep and thwart an impending horny attack. Not caught up, I was even. Still, it wouldn't do to doze off with a hard-on.

Soon, there were more guitars going down in the standby line, but I kept mine in the case. I was a professional, I figured, not a college kid anymore. Somebody was playing "Nobody Knows You When You're Down and Out," a tune I had first head from Mayo. People were snoozing everywhere, some erecting little forts around themselves made of tables and litter cans, like pioneers drawing their wagons up in a circle. I lay back, listening to a group sing-along of "I Shall Be Released," a Bob Dylan song.

Around six-thirty, the airport began coming to life, the noise level increasing, people stretching and yawning. The buffet opened where I drank a cup of coffee, adding a dollop of scotch. I talked with a girl from Chicago who said she was a TV film editor. "The Continent is so crowded," she said, "with long lines everywhere and everyone out to rip off the tourists." I didn't tell her that in Europe you didn't stand in lines, you stood in queues. An editor should have known this. The whiskey, only seventy-proof, hit me with a jolt.

Once past security, waiting in the departure lounge, I surreptitiously tried to look up the dress of an African lady sitting across from me. We had an uneventful flight to New York, arriving around eight forty-five, London time. I had a sandwich and a beer before boarding a connecting flight to Houston Intercontinental, where my mother and my pregnant wife were waiting to welcome me home.

I had been gone sixty days. Back in June, Angie had found us a new place on Twenty-Fourth Street. It was the bottom half of a two-story house, with fifteen-foot ceilings and a small back yard. It had tall windows with plenty of light. I liked it immediately, but found it hard to quit moving. Angie still had some time before school started. She was showing more and more, and I figured there wouldn't be much traveling once the baby came. One of the first things we did was pile into her car and drive to Tennessee. We arrived at Townes's place in the country; we found him laid up with a shattered arm. He had been passed out when his friend Michael had lost control going over a cattle guard and smashed into a tree.

We were back in Galveston for the dog days, with the cicadas screaming and not a trace of breeze. We got by with fans, tall cool drinks, and long siestas. Elvis Presley died in August, soon to become far more important in death than he had been his last few years on earth.

Zapata

In early October, I was back in Sugar Hill studios in Houston, working with a guy named Mickey Moody on tracks for the new record. These were outlaw sessions recorded for cash late at night and off the books. I had a few checks coming from my old job, but by November it was obvious I would have to come up with some more money. I heard that a drilling company named Zapata was hiring and filed an application one afternoon in a downtown Houston office building. Two other hands were there filling out applications. The company representative gave us a pep talk. "I guess you fellows have never heard of George Bush?" he asked.

"No sir." The two roughnecks shook their heads and looked down. I said nothing at first but I knew who he was. A Yale man, scion of wealth and privilege, former chief of the CIA, special envoy to China under Nixon . . . and president of Zapata Oil Company.

"Yeah, I know who he is," I said.

"Well, you boys are going to be hearing his name a lot."

I later wondered who this guy was, and if he went on to collect his reward in some choice political appointment after Bush became president. I also wondered why a tory like George Bush would name his company after a Mexican revolutionary. I had heard that Zapata was a slave-driving outfit, the Black Ball Line of the offshore drilling industry. But I figured it couldn't be all that bad. I figured wrong. Whereas there had been some jerks on board *Sedneth I*, it seemed that on this rig, everybody was.

The first morning, my first hour on tour, we were coming out of the hole. We had only pulled a few strands of pipe when the tip of my glove got caught up in the tongs. We pulled up another stand, and I noticed the glove was filling up with blood. I took a deep breath and yanked it off. I still had a thumb, but it wasn't pretty. The driller came by for a look. He seemed annoyed. "Better go to the medic," he said curtly. "You need to get that wrapped up."

The medic was tall and skinny. His face had a lot of miles on it without revealing much character or intelligence. I took him for a galley hand, a wine head. "It's just bruised," I said, embarrassed to be hurt my first day on the job. "I can handle it." He bandaged my thumb and I went back up to the drill floor.

I hung on for five days, working mainly with one hand. The driller, a sadistic bastard, made a point of giving me difficult things to do. One day, he put me to work cutting rusty bolts from a piece of steel plate behind the draw-works. Working with a hammer and cold chisel, each blow came with a stab of agony. Every morning we had a safety meeting, held on our own time, before we went to work. Each day I went to the medic who by now I had figured for a charlatan. I could sense that the driller wanted to get rid of me but couldn't fire me outright. Perhaps the tool pusher told him to lean on me. They wanted me to quit so the company would not have to pay workman's compensation and have a lost time accident on its record.

One day I ran into Pete, of all people, whom I had last seen back in England, and who corroborated my feelings about Zapata. "This rig sucks, man. They've only got one set of slings on board and they don't even have any air tools. They've got us chipping paint with hand scrapers, for God's sake."

My last night aboard, I was too feverish to sleep. The next morning, I could see the red lines of infection running up my arm. I went to the medic to see what he would say. I was thinking if he knew first aid, I was an atomic physicist. Sure enough, he failed to notice. "I'm getting off of here," I told him. "I need a real doctor to look at this."

I knocked on the door of the tool pusher's office and pushed it open. "I need to get on the next helicopter going ashore. My thumb is infected."

"It's your decision if you want to quit." The man looked back at some papers on his desk.

"I didn't say I wanted to quit. My thumb is infected. I need to have a doctor look at it."

"It's your decision." He didn't look up again. Back in the room I packed my things and waited in the galley. Directly I heard the *whup whup whup* of an approaching helicopter. I didn't say goodbye to anyone, there being no one around I knew or cared about. I never saw Pete again, though I talked to him on the phone once later, and learned that he drug up after his hitch was finished. When the chopper was ready to go, I threw my bag aboard and buckled up with my one good hand. "Fuck you, George Bush," I said as we lifted off.

After a forty-five minute flight to the beach, we landed at a heliport near Freeport. Thanking the pilot, I walked out by the road where I stuck out my one good thumb at the passing traffic. It took me three rides to get back to Galveston by way of the coast road and San Luis Pass. I was feverish by the time I got to the house. It was locked, but I managed to climb in through a window and collapse on the couch, where I stayed until Angie came home from school and took me to the hospital. An intern at the emergency room took one look at my thumb and gave off a low whistle.

"Is it serious?"

"You better believe it is." I was x-rayed and given a room. A nurse came by and gave me a shot, then hooked me to an I.V. bottle. I was released from the hospital three or four days later. My thumb took a long time to heal, and for a while I wondered if I would be able to play guitar again.

Bad Magic At Gilley's

"We're going to do a Richard Dobson song called 'Piece of Wood and Steel,' which was recorded by David Allan Coe. David's been telling people he comes from Texas. He comes from Texas all right. We call him a 'pussy from Coe, Texas.'"

A Hemmer Ridge Mountain Boys intro that always drew a laugh, it was probably lucky for Rex that none of David's biker buddies were ever in the audience to hear it. David had talent all right. He had gotten himself a major label record deal with CBS after writing the Tanya Tucker hit "Would You Lay With Me (In a Field of Stone)." Some people thought this song sounded a lot like Townes's "If I Needed You." I had first met David through Guy Clark after he had recorded a song of Guy's called "Desperadoes Waiting For a Train." I was thrilled when he recorded "Wood and Steel" and put it out on his second CBS album, *Once Upon a Rhyme*. In return for the favor, I had given him publishing on the song. Later, I was not so happy to see David go on to become a star while I never saw a royalty statement nor a penny of income from the record sales.

As time went by, I grew even more unhappy when I learned he was taking credit for my song. My anger turned to smoldering fury when I read his book *Just For the Record* in 1978. The cover shows David in a black hat and Nudie jacket, with earrings and an Indian necklace, all framed in motorcycle chain. The frontispiece reads, "This book is dedicated to all men in prison, be it mentally or physically, and to my children so they may know THE TRUTH!"

After a prologue in which the word *truth* is mentioned four times, David writes that "Captain John Cole was born in Essex County, England, during the reign of Edward III in the year 1440." Chapter One, "Penitentiary Blues," covers his early years in Ohio prisons and reformatories, and his biker days. Chapter Two, "Mysterious Rhinestone Cowboy," treats his early days in Nashville. And Chapter Three, "Just for the Record," describes his career at the point of taking off.

I skimmed the book up to this part, which took him to 1975, the year *Once Upon a Rhyme* came out. Then on page 153 my eyes fastened on a quote from a Billboard review: "Throughout, he is astonishingly creative, and his lyrics mark him as the Leonard Cohen of country. Like these: 'You tried to tell me what was right and I told you what was real.'" There was more to come, with David quoting a *Nashville Banner* review of March 15, 1975. "Coe ... can cut loose with some beautiful lyrics when he's a mind to: "Piece of Wood and Steel," an I-may-be-down-but-I-ain't-out salute to the musician (the title refers to his guitar), is one of his best."

Next came a quote from Dale Adamson of the *Houston Chronicle*: "His songs cut straight to the bone with the same ferocity with which he sings, 'You tried to tell me what was right and I told you what was real' in the song, 'Piece of Wood and Steel.'" Finally, David quoted the late Bob Claypool reviewing a Liberty Hall show in the *Houston Post*, "The best moments included his run-throughs of 'Piece of Wood and Steel.'"

Not only had David accepted for himself praise written for my song, but he had treated me like dirt at a show in Galveston the year before. Now, the day after I got out of the hospital, I heard he was playing Gilley's, the well-known and soon to be world famous Pasadena honky tonk. I was still hurting, wondering if my thumb would ever heal, when Angie and I arrived and took a table off to the left side of the stage. The first few rows in front were taken by bikers who formed a cordon around the stage to keep anyone else from approaching. They had a dull, menacing aura about them. I would have liked to see a fight between the bikers and Gilley's bouncer goons, with maybe a few cowboys and refinery workers thrown in. I noticed that the backstage door was also heavily guarded, but I had no reason to go there. The kind of mischief that was beginning to suggest itself to me did not require it.

After a long wait, David took the stage in his rhinestone glitter and regalia. Standing on their chairs, the bikers began to cheer and whistle. I walked back to one of the bars to get a beer. David had begun with his shtick about prison and was going into a medley of George Jones' songs and other imitations.

I returned to our table with my beer and a Coke for Angie. I had been drinking steadily all day. My smashed thumb ached all the way up my arm and I had fallen into a foul, resentful mood. There were waitresses around, but I kept going back to buy my own beers. I was on my way back for the second or third time when I found myself propelled, edging towards the mixing board. The sound wasn't much to begin with, but something strange started happening when I started happening when I started staring at the mixing-board muttering, "Fuck up! Fuck up! Fuck up!" over and over, like a mantra. I became convinced it was I who was making the sound go bad, as an eerie, wailing feedback began to fill the hall. I shifted my focus to David, repeating my mantra. The soundman was having no luck in controlling the feedback, now totally out of hand. Thus encouraged, I redoubled my efforts, trying to drill him between the eyes. Except now it was "Look up! Look up! Look up! You thieving bastard." When David looked up, the real Leonard Cohen of country shifted his beer to his injured hand and brought up his good one in the time honored classic one-finger salute. I felt a surge run through me. I might have been mistaken, but I thought David looked stricken and helpless for an instant as I directed all my pain and fury into him.

Angie looked pale and startled when I got back to the table. "I think we better go."

"Yeah, I guess you're right. Let me finish my beer."

They still had not gotten the sound back together when we left a minute later, the feedback like fiendish moans from hell. I felt a tremendous exhaustion of a kind I had never known. Years later, back in Nashville, I saw David signing autographs at Fan Fair. He was wearing a wig and looked incredibly old. I never went back to Gilley's, soon to be featured in the film *Urban Cowboy*, and I never went to see the movie either. As for what really happened that night, I have my notions, but it's not something I want to go into.

The Blessed Event

Angie's water broke just before midnight on December 21st. I drove her to the hospital with the bag she had already packed and was ready to go. Once there, I sat down in a waiting room with a half-pint of whiskey and a newspaper. We had been to a few Lamaze classes, but I had missed most of them. I didn't feel like being there, even though witnessing the birth of your child was coming into vogue then. As it turned out, the hospital staff in Galveston had not yet been converted to this notion and didn't want me in the delivery room anyway. Which was fine. Let the event remain mysterious, I thought.

Another expectant father joined me in my vigil in the waiting room, but we didn't speak. I read my paper and nipped. Directly, I heard crying down the hall, and soon after that a nurse poked her head in the door. "You can come and take a look at your son, now."

"Thanks, is everything okay?"

"Yes, everything went fine." The nurse smiled. I followed her down the hall and into the delivery room and saw that our son was red and raw and wrinkled and that his mother was okay. That was all I wanted to see.

I left as soon as I could without appearing to be in too much of a hurry. If I had expected a mystical revelation, there was none forthcoming. The morning came up cloudy as I drove down to East Beach and walked along where the waves were rolling in, as they had since time out of mind. Rolling through an unbroken continuum of days and nights, through changing tides and seasons, before Jane Long, long before the Karankawas. The Indians, who killed and reputedly ate the shipwrecked Spaniards, might have once been shipwrecked strangers themselves. Their last survivors, so the story went, had been hunted for sport by white men on Sundays after church.

I stayed a while at the water's edge watching the waves come in, thinking about all the days and nights I had spent out there working and all the busy comings and goings that in the end seemed so pointless. After a time, I drove back to the house, stopping along the way to buy a Galveston newspaper, which I intended to save and show to my son some day when he was grown.

There followed a period in my life which is not too well documented. I began writing and mailing out a series of newsletters. These were not always directly related to what was happening at the moment. Certainly the arrival of RD III in our lives was a major change. Without thinking about it, I decided to name him after my father. To please my mother, I agreed to have him baptized, though she would have been happier to have had the ceremony performed in a Roman Catholic Church. Angie's folks were nominally Lutheran, a close enough compromise, I figured. I asked JJ Wanker to stand in as godfather. I should have asked Rex, but I happened to run into JJ, who was working at his family's title business. He was going with a nice girl from Killeen and seemed like he had begun to get his life together. Also, I knew he had a suit.

How It's Done/Not Done

These events carried us on into 1979, the last year of the decade. After a period of total helplessness, RD III began moving his limbs and looking around, taking many shits, keeping us up all hours. In February, I slipped away for a couple of days at Bill's camp on the Trinity where I learned that Snuffy, who had taken to car chasing, had gotten too close to one of the wheels and had gone under. I started making notes for another newsletter about how country music was going the way of the country itself, gone, with the very landscape turning into an endless blight of strip malls and fast food joints. Real country was becoming hard to find, and so was the music.

In March, we celebrated my thirty-seventh birthday at the Gang Plank with a cake fight, slinging it all over the bar. About this time, we had Rocky Hill putting down some tracks in the studio. Brother of Dusty Hill of ZZ Top fame, he had played on my first record under the alias of Heck Doolin. Now he chose to call himself Curley Bob. A talented blues player, Rocky had trouble with the chord changes of a song called "Looking Out For Number One." Mickey Moody and I were at the mixing board in the control room and didn't realize until the next day that Rocky, a.k.a. Curley Bob, had thrown a temper tantrum. Mickey took me to the back where he had been recording. "You're not going to believe this," he said, "He broke my stool."

"Man, we should have taken this out of his pay." The stool was not just broken. It was smashed to bits.

"Well, it wasn't worth all that much."

Mickey didn't want any money for the broken stool. He was a good guy. He had offered me a chance to get a Freddy Fender cut on "Over All Over," a song I had written partly in Spanish with Freddy in mind. The catch was he wanted half of the writer's share in exchange for the deal. Mickey worked for Huey Meaux, who owned Sugar Hill Studio and produced Freddy. I had been warned to steer clear of Huey, and was just as happy he had not shown me any particular interest. I told Mickey I would think it over.

The next day, I called Guy Clark in Nashville. Townes had always been a teacher, but I didn't entirely trust him in matters of business advice. I figured Guy would give me a straight answer, and he did, "Man, you don't ever give away your writer's share for a cut."

"He's asking for half."

"Did he have anything to do with writing it?"

"No, it's all my song."

"That's not how it works."

"That's what I figured, but I wanted to ask you."

"You don't give up your writer's share to nobody. That's not how it's done."

"Thanks, Guy. I appreciate it."

I told Mickey of my decision later that night, and he shrugged. He was, like I said, a nice guy. I figured it was just the way they did business in Houston. I later found out that giving up a share of your writer's rights wasn't altogether unknown if you were talking about Elvis back in the days when he was recording.

Dada Kontrol

In the first week of April, Rex was viciously blindsided while standing at the bar at Anderson Fair, an event that nearly caused him to miss the chance of a lifetime, a concert with Lightning Hopkins at Carnegie Hall. The blow crushed his already oft-broken nose. Doctors at the VA hospital stopped the bleeding only to have it begin again the following evening, with near fatal consequences. Two days later, Rex flew to New York with gauze packed in his nose. He rented a tuxedo and played the gig, a package show with John Lee Hooker and Clifton Chenier. It was the 10th of April, and I had sent him a telegram which he still carries in his guitar case. It read DEAR REX, BREAK A NOSE.

In May, I put out another newsletter about a day in the life, getting ready for a gig up in Houston. I could play guitar again. My left thumb was a fat, ugly protuberance, but at least it worked.

Around this time, I started running with a rounder named Clyde Woodward, a dealer, hustler, and fringe character in the Houston art and music scene. Though fatally flawed, Clyde had charm and intelligence. He loved cooking and music, especially Cajun and Zydeco, and even played a little guitar, without ever quite managing to finish a song. Together we concocted a bogus art movement, a stenciled spray paint campaign called DADA KONTROL, which we carried on in Houston and on the Island. In Houston, we hit sidewalks and buildings around the Montrose area, the Contemporary Arts Museum, and Anderson Fair. We neatly stenciled a side door to the Rothko Chapel, where it was allowed to remain for years. *Webster's* defines Dada as "a movement in art or literature based on deliberate irrationality and negation of traditional artistic values" (to which we would have added *humor* as an essential ingredient). I began to see a connection between country music and Dada. Wasn't there something a little surreal about *Hee-Haw* or, for that matter, David Allan Coe prancing around like some glittering doofus bird?

Financed by the insurance settlement for my injury, work on *The Big Taste* progressed slowly through the summer of '79. We had a number of visitors to the Island, including Peter O'Brien, who had begun publishing my newsletters in the *Omaha Rainbow*. Townes stopped by with his road manager, Harold Eggers. Townes had picked up a saxophone somewhere, which he brought in from the car and proceeded to open and assemble while RD III watched, wide-eyed, from his high chair. He continued watching as Townes carefully fitted the mouthpiece and put it to his lips. Townes took a deep breath and let loose with a great honking wail. Little Richard froze in astonishment for a second then commenced screaming in terror, scowling at Townes as his mother tried to comfort him. He had another visitor that summer, Mary, who showed up one morning with her new boyfriend. I was happy to see her and glad the spell was broken, and I no longer felt any pain.

One afternoon, I went sailing on a sloop called *Gypsy* and wrote another newsletter about it. By August, with the new record mixed and my money all gone, I was once again casting about for some means of making more. Down at the docks one afternoon, I ran into Johnny Howard, and the next day I found myself out heading out the jetties again on a wooden-hulled trawler, the *Melissa*. Angie had taken me down with Little Richard, who uttered his first words, "Daddy bye-bye boat."

The *Melissa*

Dolphins were all around us when the dawn came over the water. Leaping and wheeling, breaking the surface to breathe in long, rushing sighs. With growing light, I could see twenty-five or thirty in family groups, couples, and solitaries, all feeding on the fish we'd been pushing overboard during the night. Johnny got up to stretch while I shoved another pile out through the scuppers. Johnny Howard was hard-visaged and wild-eyed as ever. The *Melissa*, sixty-seven feet overall, was perhaps twenty feet at the beam. A big dolphin with a notch in his dorsal fin passed alongside, turning effortlessly to let a sand trout pass into his mouth. Johnny spit over the rail. "Never missed a meal in your life, did you, Fucker?"

With the sun well clear of the horizon, we anchored, washing the last of the trash overboard and rinsing the three baskets of tails from the last drag of the night. Not spectacular, but not so bad either. I passed the shrimp down to Jimmy, the rig man who packed them carefully in a bed of ice. At length, he handed up a carton of eggs, a package of bacon, and three beers. Long haired and muscular, with homemade tattoos, Jimmy was not one you might call loquacious. Together we replaced the hatch cover and pulled the tarp back over it. I had planned to take a saltwater shower with the hose, but Johnny killed the engine.

Jimmy fried bacon while I rolled a joint. We drank our beers in silence, passing the joint around. Then Jimmy fried some eggs, serving them up with an enormous bowl of grits. Thinking

"Thank God the night's over," I was examining my sore hands, an action that did not escape Johnny's attention. "Ain't so easy as you remembered, breaking out again shrimping, is it? Ha ha ha."

"It's okay. You don't hear me complaining, do you?" I got up to scrape my plate. You could lose your appetite watching Johnny talk around a mouthful full of grits.

I washed up while Johnny and Jimmy retired to their bunks to study the pictures in some well-thumbed greasy magazines. I moved a foam rubber pad into the wheelhouse, preferring it to my hot and airless bunk. With the door hooked open, I had a view and a breeze. I also had a Louis L'Amour novel. The *Melissa* rocked gently at anchor. We were only a couple of miles offshore and I could just make out the new condominiums on East Beach. Just one more beer, I figured, would make things perfect.

From the cool, dim interior of the ice hold, I emerged into the blazing sunshine with a can of beer so cold it almost hurt my hand. Setting it on the deck, I turned to replace the hatch cover when, sure enough, it fell over and rolled across the deck and out the scuppers. Hanging from one of the old truck tires that served as a fender, I couldn't quite reach it. I climbed out on the dangling try-net, sinking up to my knees, the can bobbing just beyond my reach. Straining, I just managed to snatch it and scrambled back aboard, thinking how it wasn't wise to go swimming off a shrimp boat and how, contrary to popular myth, dolphins don't scare sharks away. We had been chumming all night and both nets had bites torn out of them the size of dinner plates.

Johnny and Jimmy were already asleep when I returned with my no longer so cold beer, which I never finished. I began to fall asleep, lulled by the motion of the waves, the creaking of the doors swinging from the outriggers, the slap of water against the hull, by sounds like rusty hinges, voices, the sighing of dolphins. A cockroach passed by at eyeball level. Louis L'Amour slipped from my hand.

I awoke sometime in the late afternoon, the heat of the day gone and a freshening breeze whistling through the stays, I put coffee water on the stove and went below to start the bilge pump. The one-lunger diesel chugged to life, sending a gray, scummy stream of water into the Gulf. I was back in the galley when Johnny rolled out of his bunk and walked stiffly to the rail. "Fuck you," he said affably, pulling down his shorts and positioning himself with his bottom over the rail. There wasn't much privacy on the *Melissa*.

"Back at you, Captain."

His business finished, Johnny discovered Jimmy still dead to the world and grabbed him by the foot, shaking him violently. "HEY, WAKE UP, DUMBFUCK!" Rising up on one elbow, Jimmy struggled to focus.

I fixed pork chops and mashed potatoes, cleaning the dishes afterward while Johnny and Jimmy worked patching the nets. We had not only sharks to contend with, but we'd also picked up a giant mud ball that was left where one of the big ships had anchored, as well as lumber, sunken logs, buckets, hard hats, and beer cans from around the world. According to Johnny, we stood a chance of catching a body. I knew the rule: catch a body and it went back overboard. Inform the Coast Guard and there would be no end of trouble, an investigation, and endless forms to fill out, a trip cut short, and, worst of all, the catch confiscated and destroyed. As Johnny pointed out, none of this was likely to help the man who was already dead.

We raised anchor as the sun slipped below the horizon and put out the nets as darkness began closing in. We dragged until midnight, hauling in the try-trawl every half hour. Then Johnny shut the engine down to a crawl while Jimmy and I manned the winches, bringing up the nets and making sure the cable wound on evenly. The doors came into view, collapsing together, streaming water. Jimmy set the brake and yelled to Johnny, who gave the *Melissa* full throttle. Behind us, the nets rode up in the wake, the sharks and jackfish swarming around them.

My job was to grab a twenty-foot cane pole with a hook I used to snag the lay-lines when Johnny cut the throttle. With the *Melissa* idling ahead on auto pilot, Johnny and Jimmy wound in the lines until the bags came alongside. I took another line with a hook that I attached to the bags farther back. The bags were then winched aboard one at a time, swaying above the deck. A hard yank on the slipknot and out spilled the catch. Surreal in the floodlights lay a monstrous, slithering, gasping pile of fish. Here was the object of our pursuit: shrimp. Strange translucent creatures, underwater unicorns bringing as much as seven dollars a pound. We put the nets back over and took a break for coffee before returning to a long, back-aching stretch of culling and heading the shrimp.

I took the next watch, dragging under the stars, Johnny and Jimmy sleeping, the *Melissa* surging against a light swell, Galveston lights on the horizon. Maybe, I was thinking, this wasn't so bad. I was still nervous around machinery after my roughnecking accident the year before. But to be alone again, back with the stars and lights out on the water, standing watch and listening to the static and the shrimpers chatter on the radio. There were worse ways a man might spend his time.

The Big Taste

It seemed like a dark cloud still hung over Johnny Howard, or maybe it was just the old run-down boats he captained. In any event, we lost our rudder one night and had to be towed into Sabine by the Coast Guard. To add insult in ignominy, we were fined for not having enough life preservers on board. There had to be a better way, I figured, and I determined to keep my eyes open for a better opportunity.

In October, *The Big Taste* finally came from the pressing plant. We decided on a cover design using a photo Rock had taken of me riding in a red convertible. A friend named Tom Bridges was working in a photo copy shop that had a color Xerox machine. Deciding to do our own cover, we had the albums shipped in plain white covers. We hand-glued five hundred color Xeroxes, each one slightly different, on the front, then glued the liner notes on the back. I signed and numbered them, like art prints.

Just as we had done with *In Texas Last December*, we had our album release party at Anderson Fair. Anticipating a great deal of business, I formed a company, Rinconada Incorporated, after Rinconada de Manantiales, where I had lived down in Chile in the Peace Corps. Rock designed a logo that showed a horizon of sea and sky beneath a crescent moon. It was also Rock who gave me the name of my publishing company which I'd put together at the same time, Salty Songs.

In December, I hired on with Roy Crook and Sons, a company running a fleet of offshore stand-by boats out of Freeport. It had to be easier than shrimping, I figured, and I was right up to a point. The first boat I worked on was called the *Lady Patricia*. I went on to work with the Ladies *Carol, Ester,* and *Sarah*. The work was not taxing; we stayed anchored to a buoy for days on end with little to do but look after the boat and cook for ourselves. It was a lonely existence, with just me and the captain. Some of these men liked to talk and some did not. Of these, I tended to prefer the latter, which gave me time to read. I played guitar and worked on songs, though it was always hard to find a comfortable place. I spent Christmas and New Year's Eve of 1979 offshore, and I cannot say that I minded.

I was offshore when Angie was held at knife-point by an intruder who had slipped in through our back kitchen window. He took some money and a bag of pot out of the refrigerator, but he didn't harm her otherwise. My mother gave her Rocky, a part-coyote dog, to look after her and Little Richard while I was gone. Around this time, we put some money down on a second-hand truck her father had found, a silver Ford pickup with a good camper shell.

On February 2nd, we changed crews, running in from offshore Louisiana in a snowstorm, the only time I'd ever seen snow falling on the Gulf. The boat we rode in on was called the *Trans Southern*, a sleek, powerful aluminum-hulled crew boat. I decided to try and get a job on one of these beautiful craft. I had gone from shrimp-trawler to standby boats, and now I had my eyes set on better things. A plan began to form to get my sea papers and take the Coast Guard exam for my 100-ton license. I reasoned that at least I would have something to shoot for while I toiled for wages. The idea of becoming a captain and running my own boat began to grow on me.

In March, I rented an office on the second floor of the Hendley building down on the Strand, a beautiful room with tall floor to ceiling windows of old wobbly glass. It had wainscoting and floors of virgin longleaf yellow pine. During the early days of the Civil War, an observation post had been set up on the roof of the Hendley building to watch for the arrival of the Union blockade. Beyond my door was a skylight of thick glass, which in days before electricity had helped to light the floor below. I had a couple of chairs, a desk, and a lamp. I loved my place. It spoke to me of sanity, a place to write on my days off the boat—and a refuge from the squalor and howling complaints of Little Richard.

Clyde Woodward also had a room in the Hendley building. He lived there full time. We did some carousing as well as some DADA KONTROL mischief that—this being Galveston—aroused no response whatsoever. Clyde was a charmer, a bon vivant with no agenda beyond the next good time. But he was treacherous when it came to money. Clyde had a government assistance job at the Galveston Art Center, but he always owed me money by the time payday came around. He didn't have a car and I always made a point to drive him to the bank in order to be there when he cashed his check.

I found myself tending to a growing mail order business out of my office. Thanks in no small way to Peter O'Brian who was publishing my newsletters in the *Omaha Rainbow*, I found myself filling record orders from England, Scotland, Germany, Sweden, and Australia. Perhaps there might be a chance to have the best of both worlds after all.

In April, I ran into an alcoholic boat captain named Red Beard. I had worked with him before and didn't trust him, but now he got me a job on the *Tony B*, one of the fast aluminum-hulled crew boats I had been lusting after. I didn't stay long with Red Beard, who proved to be dangerous and unreliable, drinking while running the boat. We worked out of Cove Harbor down by Rockport, then Venice, Louisiana, of all places. This was the end of the road, where the Mississippi empties into the Gulf, and where I had first started working offshore nearly twenty years before. During one of my weeks off, I recorded a single, "The Hard Way/Swamp Rat." Remembering Mayo Thompson's remark back in England, I told the drummer to play as hard as he could.

A strange line of vehicles parked by a motel caught my attention one evening when I was driving down toward the east end of the island. Closer inspection revealed it to be three custom buses and an eighteen-wheeler, all painted black. Against this background were enormous air-brushed murals of my old nemesis, David Allan Coe, in various heroic poses. There was one with him on stage, of course, and one of David on horseback at the head of a posse. There was another with David as a sort of pirate captain at the wheel of a huge power yacht. Maybe it was this last one, with David masquerading as a man of the sea, which put me over the line. I turned back around and parked. I took one of my singles with me to the motel office, where a man looked up from behind the desk. "Yes sir, can I help you?"

"Yes. Please give this to David Allan Coe. The man whose picture is on the buses outside."

"Yes sir."

"Just give this to him." I handed the clerk a copy of my record, but not before I autographed the sleeve. DEAR DAVID—DON'T GET CAUGHT LOOKING UP A DEAD DOG'S ASS.

In June I found work on another beautiful crew boat called *Alpha One*. The captain, whose name was Dave, was Cajun. Competent and steady without being overbearing about it, he was a music fan to boot. The second captain had been a bartender in New York and had acquired his sea time on yachts. I hired on in Galveston, but we were soon transferred back down to Cove Harbor, near Rockport, where we stayed the summer. John Grimaudo, an old friend and country blues guitarist, hired on as a deck hand when I was promoted to engineer. During this time *Texas Monthly* came out with a short piece about me and I gained some credibility with some folks, including my parents, who were subscribers and a little surprised, I think, to see it.

July brought more record orders from Scotland, Germany, and Japan. A song of mine called "Baby Ride Easy" was released in the United Kingdom. Recorded by Carlene Carter and the English rocker Dave Edmunds, it made the charts in London.

August to November was a dream time when we caught so

many red snapper we were able to supplement our incomes with fish we sold to the fish market. In early September, we had a hurricane party in Corpus Christi harbor, with four crew boats tied up alongside each other. I called Angie and told her to leave the Island. Some of her ancestors had survived the 1900 storm, and some were among the seven thousand or so who did not.

I've since forgotten the name of the storm, but they were still named after women then. With the bosses all gone and all the rigs evacuated, Dave found a taxi still running and brought eight or ten cases of beer back to the boat. Among the guys we partied with were some of the crew of *The Poet*, a small freighter out of New York, a ship that was lost in the Atlantic a few years later with all hands aboard. These were good days, living on the water, fishing every chance we got, and playing music in my time ashore.

I put out another newsletter in October about Skinny Dennis and my worst job ever, working for Manpower in Nashville back in 1972. Then the *Alpha One* was transferred to Intracoastal City, Louisiana, and thing began to change. One afternoon, the second captain, Blake, lost a fish while I was at the wheel, a big ling, and I believe from this point on, he began to nurse a grudge.

Trouble

Intracoastal City was a bummer. We had to navigate a crowded ditch with a series of locks to get offshore. It was some ten or fifteen miles long and there was no more spare time for fishing. I missed Cove Harbor and Rockport with its wind-sculpted live oaks, sparking bay waters, and sandy beaches. Intracoastal City lay surrounded by marsh and flat horizons. There were docks, pipe yards, oilfield supply houses, and a couple of bars. It was not a friendly place. My truck was even towed one night for being parked in the wrong lot.

One night running in, we hit something, punching a grapefruit-sized hole in the bow just below the waterline. Another boat radioed to tell us we were running strangely, driving the bow under. I went below and figured how to pump out the forepeak, which may have saved us from sinking.

It was early December when Blake came on board after an evening of drinking ashore. I had noticed a certain coolness developing between us but ignored it, figuring he was short-tempered from working too much straight time. I thought he had needlessly bulled my friend John Grimaudo, but John was gone and it was none of my business. I was watching TV with Pete, the deckhand. It appeared that the Houston Oilers were finally beating Pittsburgh, shutting them down 6 to 0, when Blake came into the galley.

"I need to talk to you alone," he said, the tone of his voice causing Pete to make a hasty exit.

"What's the deal?" I remembered that Dave was off the boat, probably at the dispatchers shack. Blake had chosen his moment well. He was lisping.

"You've been getting too fucked up."

"Looks to me like you're the one who's fucked up."

"That's right. You been getting fucked up all the time."

"Bullshit." I had never trusted Blake. I distrusted the fact that he used to wear khaki and had got his sea time working on yachts. I suspected he liked to imagine himself as some kind of naval officer. I was annoyed and taken off guard.

"I've seen you hanging out, sneaking booze in the parking lot."

"Listen here, what I do off the boat is my business. If you don't like it you can shove it, you phony bastard. You were at the wheel the other night and didn't even know we were sinking—and get off my goddamned back!"

Blake rose up out of his seat and I hit him. Some 220 pounds and ten years my junior, he ducked my first blow, which crashed into his temple. I knew I was in trouble when I put everything I had into a left that sent him back a foot or two. All I had done was stun him. Within seconds, I found myself in a headlock, still with one arm free, pounding him in the stomach. Things went from bad to calamitous when he got hold of my hair and threw me to the galley floor. Still holding on to my hair, he began to knee me in the head.

From far away I could hear myself screaming, "Okay! I quit, motherfucker. Just let me get my things and I'm gone," but he kept on. Struggling to retain consciousness, lights exploding in my brain, I experienced an eerie lucidity: Would he stop, or was I going to have to go for the butcher knife in the drawer above my head? I knew exactly where it was, and a long time passed before he quit pounding me.

I pissed him off one more time while I was packing my stuff. He came at me like a train, arms windmilling. I shut the door on him, pinning his arm and threw all my weight against it while he bellowed like an enraged bull. I never quit cussing him—I wouldn't be denied the pleasure. Things died down for a minute and I managed to get my bag, cassette player, and my Martin off the boat. Pete, who hadn't been much help earlier, rounded up the rest of my things. Dave had also come back by this time and was hoping to smooth things over by asking me to come back aboard.

"No way, man. I can't work with him, not after this. I could never turn my back on him."

"Look, why don't you come on back and we'll talk this over."

"I can't do it, Dave. That's one sorry son of a bitch."

Dave paused for a second. "Yeah, I know that, but I can handle it. You see, I ain't torn between two lovers."

I slept in my truck until daylight. Heading back to Galveston, my hands were so swollen I could barely touch the wheel. I was passing through Beaumont when I heard Carlene Carter and Dave Edmunds singing "Ride Baby Easy" on the radio. I had trouble getting my hand in my pocket to get a quarter out to call the station and thank them for playing my song. The next Saturday, I went down to Houston to hear John Grimaudo at Anderson Fair. It was good to see him on stage after taking all that shit on the boat. Then John Lennon got shot dead in New York.

The small Asian man behind the counter looked distressed to see my grief-stricken face as I placed a six-pack of beer on the counter and handed him some money. "Will that be all, sir?"

"John Lennon is dead."

"I'm sorry sir." He pronounced it *solly*.

"I said John Lennon is dead. Don't you know who John Lennon is?"

"I'm solly, sir."

Somehow I felt that he should have known that even though John Lennon was not American, his death was important. If this man was going to be over here running a convenience store, he ought to know that a great man is gone. With tears running freely down my face, I took a piece of paper and wrote it down for him: JOHN LENNON IS DEAD.

I handed him the paper and walked out with my beer.

We didn't have any Beatles or John Lennon records back at our place. I had a three-album Neil Young retrospective called *Decade* and I put one on the turn table and cranked it up loud enough to shake the house. I figured Lennon would have dug the choice all right. I drank my beer and smoked a fat joint. Weeping, I vowed to return to music full time.

Home Owners

Sometime in January of 1981, Angie and I bought a little bungalow on Avenue S, down the street from her parent's house. She picked it out and my dad helped put up the money for a down payment. I had to give up my loft at the Hendley building. "You'll have an office in the house," she said, and I knew it was the beginning of the end.

Despite my resolution to go back to music, I soon found myself working for another boat company. Although I would hang on a little longer in Galveston, I hated the new house. I hated having to give up my office in the Hendley building. My father-in-law used to barge in at any moment unexpectedly. He was a boor, which was nothing remarkable in itself, but one day he went too far. I had just come in off the boat and was looking for my paycheck, which I knew had arrived. I turned to Angie. "Have you seen my check? I know it's come and I can't find it."

"Oh, Daddy took care of it for you."

"He what?"

"He deposited it in the bank for you."

I turned to her in disbelief. "What gives him the right to open my mail? Did he endorse it for me too?"

"I don't know. He was only trying to do you a favor."

"Well, he's not doing me any kind of favor opening my mail."

Storming out of the house, I slammed the door behind me. The place was a mess. My slim, dark-eyed schoolteacher had become a dispirited housewife. In the evenings she smoked and watched

M*A*S*H on television. I washed the dishes when I was at home, otherwise, they'd pile up. Most of the boats I worked on now were so clean you could have eaten off the floor. You couldn't say that about our house.

The kid was okay. I didn't mind looking after him in the mornings. We had a rubber hose attached to the spout in the bath tub where I used to take him in and hose him off, washing the shit off his ass while he squealed and giggled from the cold water. Around noon I would take him to his grandparents' place down the street.

I have no recollection of my thirty-ninth birthday. Perhaps I was offshore. In May, the tenth annual Kerrville Folk Festival rolled around. I had started hanging out in Austin with songwriters Danny Epps, Blaze Foley, and Rich Minus, all talented guys with a serious bent for honky-tonk living. I put out another newsletter and shortly afterward received a nasty note from Rod Kennedy, the festival promoter. I had mentioned drugs in reference to the festival and thoughtlessly mailed him a copy. Clearly, I had never learned the so-called art of tact or diplomacy. Years would pass before I was ever invited to play there.

But it was Kerrville that had once again set the stage for a major change in my life. Driving back to Austin by way of Luckenbach, Rich Minus and I shared a good laugh. I had been hanging out and shared some mushrooms with a woman who ran a primate center up in Norman, Oklahoma. "Man, you're not gonna believe this, but I ran into this woman who acts like a chimpanzee when she's drunk. You know: *Huh, Huh, Huh, Huh.*"

Rich exploded, wheezing and bending over double and we nearly ran off the road. I could sense impending change building like a knot in my stomach.

Early in September, I drove to Nashville by way of Norman, where the chimp lady was winding up her affairs. In Nashville I stayed with Bob Oermann, a writer who worked for the Country Music Foundation. I saw old friends John Lomax, David Onley, and Hugh Moffatt. I met John Prine, who had moved to town, and a pretty young singer named Kathy Mattea. In fact, a whole fresh scene had sprung up in Nashville with new generations of songwriters having moved to town to make a go of it. I figured it was time I moved back, but first there was unfinished business in Texas.

The lady primatologist was hanging out in Houston at Anderson Fair and one thing led to another in the way that these things happen. I had found some white-face backstage and painted myself up like an aborigine the night Angie came to repossess the truck. She came with her big brother, a glowering hulk with short arms. She was dragging Little Richard along with her and wasn't amused with the white-face.

"Why do you have that stuff all over your face? You look ridiculous."

"You probably wouldn't understand."

"There's a lot of things I don't understand."

"I suppose you don't."

"I need the keys."

I had to go on in a few minutes, so I gave her the keys. Angie scattered my things all over the sidewalk in front of the club and left with the kid. The truck was in her name anyway, but it wasn't such a good move on her part. Taking it back only made me more dependent on the chimp lady, who eventually moved with me back to Nashville on April Fool's Day, 1982.

Old Wood

In December, back before I'd left the Island, I happened to stop by and visit my friend Jim Studebaker at his shop down near the Strand. An artist and woodworker who specialized in restoring nineteenth century homes and furniture, Jim and I shared an interest in boats and had gone out sailing a couple of times. I found him busy working in his shop, but not so busy that I didn't find him amenable to go out for a jug of wine.

A pungent smell of resin hit us when we re-entered the room, which was covered with a film of sawdust. It was about twenty feet deep and three times as long, with shelves full of old lumber rising along the back wall. There was a high ceiling, twelve feet or more, with a massive workbench on the near wall. A variety of tools hung above it: old time planes, chisels, and draw knives. A radial saw and two suspended window fans, some lights, and a small radio appeared to be the only concessions to the modern age.

I noticed a familiar art piece leaning against the all, a Richard Mock print. Richard had had a show in Galveston the year before.

"Haven't I seen it somewhere?"

"I'm making a new frame for it. The old one was starting to warp." The print belonged to a mutual friend who had brought it in. Jim showed me a piece of straight-grained, honey colored wood he had been shaping. It felt dense, heavier than it should have been, and it gave off a sharp smell of resin.

"What kind of wood is this?"

"Isn't it beautiful?"

"It's really nice."

"This is a long-leaf yellow pine, original growth. It came out of the Bloom building across the alley."

"Then it was cut over a century ago?"

"Probably in the 1850s, maybe much earlier." Jim wiped the dust from a pair of glasses while I uncapped the wine. He explained that most of pre-1900 Galveston was built with yellow pine brought by ship from the East Coast, where it was abundant as far up as the Carolinas. The needs of the frontier Texas community were meager, but ships arriving for cotton needed cargo for ballast. Lumber was the answer of how to fill empty hulls in the east-west trade. The wood from the Bloom building was cut and dragged to a sawyer, probably by ox team. There, it was rough cut and cured for two to three years before it was shipped.

"How old do you figure the tree was?"

"Well, let's see." Jim took a set of calipers from the wall and measured the cross grain of the piece he had just cut. "Let's see, this has twenty growth rings to the inch. This particular piece looks like it was cut fairly close to the center of the tree. I'd say the tree was probably six feet in diameter, so it was about 1,440 year old when it was cut down.

"You're kidding." I reached for a pencil. "You're saying the tree this wood came from was growing around 541 A.D.?"

"It was in the ground up to ten years before it even sprouted."

I tried to imagine the primordial scene this tree must have been part of, long before the coming of the white man. I asked if any virgin yellow pine still existed. Jim said he thought there were a few stands left, possibly in the Big Thicket. When I asked why the builders didn't cut their lumber from the Big Thicket in the first place, Jim said that lumbering didn't get started in East Texas until the 1800s or 90s, by which time most of the Strand construction had already been completed.

We had smoked a joint earlier, which, combined with the wine sent me thinking of time loops, of the intersection of our lives with these impossible contingencies. A fourteen hundred year old tree rendered into a nineteenth century wall stud. Recycled now into a frame for this late-twentieth century art: a block print of a dog with a woman's leg in its mouth.

Jim and I kept refilling our glasses until the wine was gone. I left him there still shaping pieces for the frame. A couple of days later, I happened to see the print hanging on the wall at our friend's house. I took it down and turned it around to see how the work had turned out. Jim had done a fine job, the corners perfectly mitered and fit with diagonal bracing. A shiver ran through me as I felt the ancient, holy wood and inhaled its resin.

The Bear

The bear moved out across the ice, ignoring the dog barking at his heels. He was a young male and had lived with his mother. It had always been so, until one day she turned snarling at him with a sudden unexplained ferocity. He followed at a distance for two days in brute bewilderment but always she turned back on him with renewed fury until he finally went on alone.

The weather turned to freezing as he headed south, wandering across a vast expanse of frozen marsh until he came to the coast. Hungry, he found a great number of fish dead or moving sluggishly and these sustained him as he moved on down the peninsula. He had passed well to one side of the women's camp when the dog was alerted. The bear had never seen ice before but moved confidently across the frozen bay towards the opposite shore.

He passed close by the charred remains of Laffite's camp, torched by the decamping buccaneers the year before. On the next day, he came upon the camps of the Karankawa, the circle of holes where the wickiup poles had stood, and he paused sniffling at the cold dead ashes in the middle. There was nothing left save some bits of shell and bone and, down by the shoreline, the marks where their dugouts had been pulled up in the mud Prairie wolves had been there before and it is not likely that they themselves had found much to scavenge.

The bear moved on under chevrons of duck and geese, and a great flock of sandhill cranes rose up before him and settled again where he had passed. Replete with fish, he felt no hunger.

He felt no urge to hibernate and would not likely have found a suitable place even had he wanted to. In the afternoon, he came to the end of the Island. A line of surf washed beyond the ice that covered the pass. He broke through the ice and swam until he clambered back up at a place where it would hold him. He shook, his rippling fur sending off a showering cascade of freezing droplets, then moved on.

Post Script

Rex and Mary Daily split up sometime in 1978. The Hemmer Ridge Mountain Boys continued to play until 1980, when Rex married a woman named Sharon and moved to Long Island, New York. He worked there for a time making windmill generators with his father-in-law. When they returned, Rex played in another band called the Louvers that lasted until the guitar player and Rex's wife ran away together to California. No longer married, Rex doesn't drink much these days, at least that's what he'll have you believe. Hats off to him, though. He did put on a coat and tie for a few years. He saved his money and bought his beach house out on Bolivar, just a few miles from the ferry landing where Jane Long, her daughters, and her slave, Kian, endured that terrible winter long ago.

Jane Long gave birth to another daughter, and later was known for many years as the first white woman to give birth in Texas. The women were eventually rescued by a passing party of settlers in the summer of 1822. A pioneer woman of considerable fortitude, Jane outlived her children, dying in 1880 at the age of eighty-three. She was known to smoke a pipe and wear a homespun dress and palmetto-leaf hat. Of her filibustering husband James, he is said to have grown despondent on the eve of his death in Mexico when he told his companion, "Milam, I have a presentiment I shall never see my family again. Promise me you will take care of them."

The Karankawas who came back to frighten the desperate

women did not stay long on the Island. Ravaged by European diseases against which they had no defenses, they did not survive the rapid advance of a new wave of settlers. Greatly reduced in number, there were still a few Karankawas living in the area of Rockport where the daughter of a ship captain, Alice William Oliver, made the only known study of their language. By the late 1850s, they had all but disappeared. In 1963, a Karankawa grave site was unearthed during construction of Jamaica Beach on West Galveston Island.

Before archeologists could arrive, the locals had set up a sign on the highway that read: INDIAN GRAVES—DIG FREE. A hot dog stand was set up on the spot to feed the grave robbers and the curious.

Rex and I have often wondered what became of Johnny Howard. Rex almost had me convinced he might have drowned by now, but I'm not so sure. There's still a lot of shrimp in the Gulf and I'd like to think Johnny's still out there in some leaky old trawler dragging for them.

Mickey White has been sober since 1983. He lives outside of Austin where he is raising his son, John. JJ Wanker sold the Blue Unit not long after coming back off the road. He dropped out of the title business after his mother died, and moved to Palacios down on the coast where he lived for several years. He has since come back to the Island. After a couple of close calls, he lives with the certainty that he must stay sober or die. The last I heard of Chito, he had joined the Navy and had become a drug and alcohol counselor. Blaze Foley was shot and killed in Austin in 1988. After living in Los Angeles for a number of years, Clyde Woodward died of cirrhosis of the liver in 1992. Holly James remarried and gave birth to two daughters. Mary Dillon died of a heart attack in 1994, not long before her fortieth birthday.

Townes and Cindy broke up in 1980. He moved back to Austin, where he married a woman named Jeanene. She bore him two children, Will and Katie Belle. Through many crises and dry-out spells in the hospital, his legend continued to grow, even as his strength diminished. Back in Nashville once again, Townes toured constantly. Though often too sick to play, he did better on the road than he did at home. He continued to write and record, and he worked in Europe a lot. His old friend and road manager Harold Eggers stayed working with him to the end. Townes suffered delusions and lived constantly with ghosts, spirits, and hallucinations. Being around him was frequently an exhausting ordeal. It was like when you hear the neighborhood dogs start howling in pain from an ambulance siren—only with Townes those sirens never stopped wailing and his pain never ceased. It was the pain of his existence, no less, and he dealt with it the best he could.

Townes was living by himself in Guy and Susanna Clark's old house in Mount Juliet when I went back for a visit in March of 1996. I noticed an award on the dresser with a plaque that read:

> KERRVILLE MUSIC AWARD
> KERRVILLE FOLK FESTIVAL HALL OF FAME
> TOWNES VAN ZANDT

I hefted the award and set it back down. "How in the world did you rate this?"

Townes demurred. "I don't know. They had some kind of election. I was on the road in Germany at the time. Jeanene picked it put for me."

"Well, congratulations."

"Thanks. I guess it's an honor. It's really nice of them and all—" Townes' trailed off in thought.

"It's funny. You're still getting yourself elected—do you remember that winter up in Jackson in the Blue Unit when you had yourself elected the 'nicest and most considerate person among us'?"

"Yeah." Townes smiled and shook his head. "Those were some times."

"Those were some cold times."

"It's a miracle we survived."

I picked up the award once again. "It's funny. You know: for all of Rod Kennedy's preaching against drugs and rowdy behavior down through the years, you epitomize everything he's against. All the gambling, pot smoking, boozing, and carousing—you're the main inspiration behind all of it."

Townes smiled again. "Yup, I know it. I know it and I'm proud of it, too."

It was John Lomax who phoned with the news about Mary, and I took her death hard. I could sort of understand the others, or at least see how they had helped bring it on themselves. On the morning of her funeral, I happened to see Rodney Crowell in the Kroger parking lot. I had just pulled in some distance away when I watched him get in his car with an armload of flowers and drive off. But when I got back to the house and checked Mary's obituary, there was a request that said PLEASE, NO FLOWERS. I figured it was a coincidence, seeing Rodney, and that he must have been buying flowers for somebody else.

Bolivar Redux

As for this story, I'm sure some will claim to remember parts of it differently. Like all stories, it is filtered through the lens of perception, altered by time and the lapses to which memory is prone. And while it concerns real people, it was never intended as autobiography or memoir. Events and chronology have been shuffled, and some names and situations are inventions. Early on I intended to call this work a novel, and that is the word that best describes my intentions. Perhaps it doesn't matter what you call the dog, so longs as the dog will hunt. We all choose some kind of fiction to project upon the world, and this is one of them. But for all that, this is a true story—at least I've tried to make it so.

If I may speak for all of us, I can offer no excuse or apology for the way we lived. To an extent, we were products of our time. It would not play today, nor is it the kind of life I would recommend to anyone. Those days, *los dias que ya no son*, are constantly receding behind us. As for what I've learned, I've seen peaks and valleys, some hard-won triumphs and gut-twisting despair. But more and more these have become the tribulations of a man finally grown—a continuation certainly, but another story with the youth gone out of it. Life goes on for those of us lucky enough to have survived.

The music goes on, too. The music goes on; it lives in us and sustains us. Speaking just for myself, I've left much of my anger behind, and for this alone I would consider it all an even trade.

Townes Van Zandt passed away in Nashville on January 1, 1997. Though we spoke on the phone the week before he died, the last time I saw him alive was at Rex's club, the Old Quarter in Galveston. This was one of his last gigs in America, and the last time I ever opened a show for him. It was early in October 1996, and unusually high tides were inundating the coast, threatening the first line of beach houses. Townes looked unreal; he had become so frail and thin. I had the impression his spirit was already beginning to leave his body. Though Rex said he thought Townes played well, I was not so sure and was filled with disquiet. I was on my way to Nashville the next morning, so I didn't stay at the club until closing time.

Tides were still way up when I drove to the ferry and crossed over to Boliver on the old *E.H. Thornton Jr.* I stopped at Rex's house where I knew Townes and Harold were staying, but they weren't there. Thinking perhaps it was just as well, I drove on up the coast road. Passing through Crystal Beach, I saw Townes' truck parked at the Outrigger Grill, alongside Rex's. I slowed down to make a U-turn, but after a second's hesitation, I drove on up to High Island, north to Winnie, and then east on I-10 to Beaumont, Orange, Lake Charles, Lafayette, and Baton Rouge. I knew the way by heart, for I had passed through there many times before.—RD, 1998

1998–Special Thanks

Among the people who have helped in the preparation of this manuscript, I would like to thank the following for their helpful comments and suggestions: Roxy Gordon, John Lomax III, Joe Nick Patoski, Peter Blackstock, Mark "Sergio" Webb, and especially, Danny "Ruester" Rowland for invaluable assistance with revisions.

I would also like to thank Pat Cleere, Sherry Raeigle, and Stephan Jarrard for their assistance in proofreading the final galley proofs. Thanks also to my neighbor, LeAnne Romano, for cling to my rescue on those frequent occasions when I could not make my computer work, and to Edith for love and patience.

This book is dedicated to my parents, whose love and support has already been there.

                    Richard J. Dobson
                    Jamaica Beach, Texas. January, 1998.

Printed in Great Britain
by Amazon